OSCAR ROMERO

A MAN FOR OUR TIMES

JULIO O. TORRES

Seabury Books
NEW YORK

Seabury Books
19 East 34th Street
New York, New York 10016

www.churchpublishing.org

An imprint of Church Publishing Incorporated

Cover photograph by Victor Manuel Villaran Lopez; used by permission.
Cover design by Marc Whitaker, MTWdesign
Typeset by PerfecType, Nashville, Tennessee

A record of this book is available from the Library of Congress.

ISBN: 978-1-64065-349-8 (paperback)
ISBN: 978-1-64065-350-4 (ebook)

To my mentors and Jesuit martyrs
of the Salvadoran civil war:
Ignacio Martin Baro, Segundo Montes,
and Ignacio Ellacuría

And to my children:
Javier, Elisa, Natalie, Pablo, Orlando, Noah,
and Julio Esteban

CONTENTS

INTRODUCTION

Rarely is a biographer given the chance to examine the life of a person of heroic proportions from the standpoint of his close contemporaries and direct personal knowledge. I was graciously afforded this opportunity when I undertook the task of writing this psychobiography of martyred archbishop Oscar Romero.

This work is an attempt to understand and uncover the humanity of one of the most important religious figures of the twentieth century. In my research, I found out that it is quite remarkable how quickly a person—Romero in this case—can become a myth and be elevated to a supernatural realm. Prophets and saints are usually confined to a special kind of Olympus, but they were also ordinary human beings. New Testament scholars have labored for centuries to find the "historical" Jesus, a task that has turned out to be quite difficult due to the time separating us from him, along with the myriad factors in between. However, because of the proximity of Romero's existence, I was in a much better position to approach the humanity of a saint, as he was proclaimed by the Salvadoran people long before he was canonized by the Roman Catholic Church. I hope to look at the *historical* Romero as a model for emulation, and to appreciate the quality of his achievement and its significance for our time.

This psychobiography was based on primary and secondary sources. I met Romero when he was still an auxiliary bishop. I was a lay member of JEC (Christian Student Youth). Ironically, in retrospect, he was one of the organizers of a crusade aimed at persuading families to pray the Roman Catholic Rosary. It was around 1970, and a devastating civil war was brewing in El Salvador. At first sight, Romero was simply a pious and quiet clergyman; in fact, he appeared to be rather shy and spoke very little. I don't remember anything he said. His presence at JEC was mainly to support our efforts. He was just there. Romero was not known as a people's advocate, but as a conservative bishop, and a staunch one at that, which made his change of course—some would say conversion— even more spectacular. Twenty years after his death, I traveled to El Salvador four times between September 2000 and August 2004 to conduct interviews that became my primary sources. I interviewed all of Romero's surviving relatives, friends, and coworkers—mainly clergy. Being a Salvadoran-born American and a priest greatly helped in opening doors and facilitating the interviews. Most people I interviewed appeared interested in the project and were open and candid; I was a *padre* and they trusted me. For the most part they did not conceal their biases in their evaluation of Romero and the admiration, awe, or even deadly hatred that he inspired in them. They shared a great deal of their time, sometimes an entire day, to help my research.

Introduction

My interviews were free-floating and informal. I simply took notes and refrained from using a tape recorder to respect the wishes of the interviewees and foster their spontaneity. I began by explaining that I was trying to understand Romero as a human being—not a religious public figure but a flesh and blood person—in order to bring him closer to us. My questions loosely followed the order below, with variations to allow for the flow of the interviewee's associations:

- When did you meet Monsignor Romero?
- What was your relationship to him, and how long did it last?
- What kind of person was Monsignor Romero? How would you describe him? (Often I had to prompt people on this point to talk of Romero as a human individual, setting aside the religious *transference*.[1])
- What do you remember the most about Monsignor Romero? Tell me a story. (In the case of people who knew him as a child or as a young man I would ask more pointed questions about his upbringing and education.)
- Anything else you would like to tell me about him? (This last part was usually the longest, since I allowed ample time for free associations.)

My interviews covered a wide range of people including his three surviving brothers, his sister, clergy and lay associates, as well as his closest friend, a traveling salesman with whom I traveled for days at a time. I will refer to them specifically and describe them in detail as they appear in the narrative.

To speak of psychoanalysis as a biographical tool may elicit misgivings about the so-called imperialistic role of psychoanalysis when it purported to be an all-encompassing way of understanding humanity and society. We have come a long way since Professor William Langer's famous challenge to the American Historical Association in 1957, when he advocated the use of psychoanalysis as a tool for furthering our understanding of history. The role of psychoanalysis is now understood as more modest but still essential. Robert Jay Lifton writes:

> There is a real paradox here, important to keep in mind particularly in historical and cultural studies: without psychoanalysis, we don't have a psychology worthy of address to history and society or culture. But at the same time, if we employ psychoanalysis in its most pristine form, we run the risk of eliminating history in the name of studying it. . . . [M]ost of history is eliminated in the name of individual psychopathology. . . . Erik Erikson is a key figure in what might be called a new wave of psychohistory. . . . What Erikson managed to do was to hold psychoanalytic depth while immersing himself in the historical era being studied and then relating those currents to that figure.[2]

Erik Erikson's seminal work on Luther was one of the main inspirations for this work. He did a masterly analysis of the relationship between personality, historical context, and social and theological impact in the life of the religious genius of the

Introduction

Reformation. He created the model of *the great individual in history*,[3] a model in which the person under study is placed in their concrete historical context and the influences of the latter on their personality and actions are thoroughly considered. We must, however, leave room for *the irreducible*,[4] that which cannot be explained by any theory, psychological or otherwise, that which is beyond words, and can only, perhaps, be half-way described, as the action of the divine Spirit.

Psychohistory is an essential tool for historians because it adds a new dimension to the interpretation of history. In addition to the social, political, and narrative aspects, the clinical art of psychoanalysis can shed light on the emotional forces that propelled individuals to act in response to their historical context. Instead of appealing to the common-sense explanation, or leaving great lacunae as far as the emotional motivations of the person under study are concerned, psychohistory allows the researcher to add a new layer of interpretation and prediction to their task.

The psychoanalytic method places the observer in a particular mix of identification and detachment. The subjective aspect is a novel contribution in the sense of bringing our own feelings and responses, attitudes, behaviors, fantasies, attractions, and aversions into play through the phenomena of transference and counter-transference,[5] which then becomes an added tool and asset for understanding. The psycho-biographer strives to empathize fully with the individual and period and establish an emotional interpretive communication that is as immediate as possible with regard to the past. The psycho-biographer must allow their "evenly suspended" attention to become a more precise focus on the resonant themes and facts that lead to interpretation. The psycho-biographer does not disregard the forces of aggression, libido, fantasies, slips, passions, and peculiarities that may be overlooked by a classical historian.

Unlike Freud, who suggested that the human personality was largely determined by age five, Erikson saw human development taking place throughout the entire life of the individual in eight stages, which he called epigenetics, after the scientific term related to the doctrine that the entity that will develop into a viable system is acted upon and depends on both the conditions in its environment and its internal coding. In Erickson's view the same holds true in terms of personality development. The human individual is equipped to continue to grow, given the right conditions, until life comes to an end. The method for applying psychoanalytic theory to Archbishop Romero's historical material was carried out in three stages: *reading* primary and secondary materials in a comprehensive way; *noting* words or incidents that appear most relevant; and *analyzing* the materials selected to better understand the individual's motivations and behavior patterns. Romero's diaries and sermons, along with the firsthand witnesses' interviews, constitute the primary material. Other works cited constitute the secondary materials and are listed in this book's bibliography.

The interviews were carried out in Spanish and I relied on my translation of them to incorporate them into the corpus of the entire work. The interviews turned out to be the richest and most novel materials because they are eyewitness accounts registered solely by me. Thus, I was able to capture the emotional texture of the stories and statements. The secondary materials, were, for the most part, originally written in Spanish. I compared my own translation with the authorized translation of the materials, when available, and will point out any significant differences.

I had to choose portions or incidents in the materials that stood out as revealing of a particular psychological or historical influence in the archbishop's life. I have also included an explanation of my choices of particular factors and events. This approach must necessarily be reductive, but not reductionistic. By reductive I mean I had to single out some elements from the entire corpus and exclude others. I wanted to analyze all the relevant factors until I arrived at a plausible unified view of the interface between psychological and historical factors and their impact on Romero's life. I summarize my responses in a postscript. I do not attempt to use my own responses to prove a particular point, but they are helpful and revealing in terms of the effect Romero had on other people.

To date no *psycho-biographical* study of Archbishop Romero has been attempted. This work aims at becoming a novel and welcome contribution to the growing field of Romero studies. A fledgling center has been erected for this purpose at the Jesuit university in San Salvador, Central American University (known as UCA El Salvador). The Jesuit fathers graciously allowed me to have access to the wealth of books and documents contained there, as well as to the adjacent museum where I could see the relics, the bloody cassock with a bullet hole being the most striking element on display.

As a native of El Salvador, a Jesuit alumnus, and a clergyman, I believe I was particularly well suited to undertake this project. I was brought up in the same cultural and religious environment as the archbishop and, before I became an Episcopalian, I attended the same Roman Catholic seminary as Romero. There, I became intimately familiar with the religious ideology and training prevalent in Romero's time. I also lived through several dictatorships and was acquainted with the prevalent climate of repression and human rights violations. My aim is to contribute to the understanding of how Romero's radical transformation came about while emphasizing the human traits that make him more accessible to us, as an inspiration in our struggle for human rights and the gestation of a prophetic spirituality for our times.

CHAPTER 1
WAYS OF SEEING ROMERO

Latin American Liberation Theology

In order to understand Romero's evolution as both person and priest, we need to become acquainted with the intellectual religious phenomenon known as Latin American liberation theology, not just because this movement influenced Romero greatly, but also because he came to be regarded as one, if not the foremost, embodiment of it. As early as the 1960s the ferment began in El Salvador with groups of students, workers, teachers, university professors, and peasants gathering to reflect on the Bible in the light of current affairs, and conversely to look at reality in the light of Holy Scripture. Traditional Church teachings were being reinterpreted in the light of the emerging socioeconomic reality.

Revolutionary movements were underway in most of the continent, and Central America had become a kind of testing ground for the geopolitical ambitions of the Soviet Union and the United States. In the late sixties and early seventies, populist governments like those of Cardenas in Mexico, Peron in Argentina, and Vargas in Brazil had been able to transform import substitution economies by creating manufacturing industries at home that produced the commodities that formerly had to be purchased from industrialized countries. This economic switch gave rise to a significant industrial working class but plunged the peasantry into even greater destitution.

Unskilled workers and their families swelled the periphery of the main capital cities, dwelling in shantytowns under the most inhuman and unsanitary conditions, without sewers, running water, or electricity. Because of the high hopes placed by Latin Americans on Kennedy's Alliance for Progress, its failure to improve the living conditions of the majority also contributed to a wave of popular despair. President Kennedy was so revered by the poor that you could see in many humble dwellings an image of him alongside of Jesus and other saints on the household altar, illuminated by candles. Most Latin American thinkers realized that development was impossible under the aegis of dependent capitalism. Structural change was needed. The *aggiornamento*[1] proposed by the Second Vatican Council gave an impetus to Latin American theologians, many of whom were pastors and served in marginal communities, to rethink traditional Christian teaching.

The influence of Marxist intellectuals was also relevant in prompting the new theologians, many of whom had been educated in Europe, where Marxism was already integrated into sociological thought. Liberal theologians used historical materialism[2] as a tool to analyze social reality. Most liberation theologians would agree with the Marxist dictum that "hitherto philosophers have explained the world. Our task is to change it." Classical theology reflects on Church tradition and Holy Scripture in order to explain their meaning for our times and thus deduce ethical norms. Liberation theology analyzes personal and historical events first in order to formulate a proper Christian response to them, which it calls *praxis* (πρᾶξῐς), or liberating practice.[3]

The tables were turned. The understanding of praxis as a concrete response to historical reality took precedence over abstract reflection, which came to be considered the second movement of theologizing. In fact, there was a good deal of reflection taking place in rural and workers' communities through the lens of European political theology.[4] Understanding society in terms of class struggle made a great deal of sense to those living in a society sharply divided into classes. Students, workers, peasants, intellectuals, and progressive people in general longed for the kind of egalitarian societies we learned about through exiles, literature, and the media.

The new reading of the Bible propounded by liberation theologians felt like a breath of fresh air and, above all, it seemed to fit in perfectly with the reality of the social destitution we had to witness daily. We were influenced mainly by European theologians like the humanist Jacques Maritain, the personalist Emmanuel Mounier, Teilhard de Chardin's theology of evolution, Yves Congar's work on the ministry of the laity, and Ivan Illich's critique of the institutional Church. Brazilian educator Paulo Freire's pedagogical approach, known as *concientizacion* (roughly "consciousness-raising" in English), was also highly influential and revolutionized popular education.[5]

All of the above thinkers had something in common: they were heirs to the Enlightenment thought that placed the human being at the center of things—even at the cost of eliminating God. In terms of Catholicism this meant, among other things, giving a new role to the laity and fighting clericalism. Those of us who had been raised in traditional Catholicism were taught to place God at the center of all things, to revere the clergy and heed their advice. Romero was also a child of this kind of theology; accordingly, he was protective of the clergy's traditional role and suspicious of humanistic social movements.

As a part of my research, I visited the rural community of Santa Marta in the province of Sensuntepeque in El Salvador. In the mid-eighties, the people of Santa Marta migrated to neighboring Honduras en masse, running away from the Salvadoran army's "scorched-earth"[6] policy. The killing, execution style, of six Jesuit priests at the Catholic university (UCA) in 1989 and the takeover of the capital city of San Salvador by the guerrillas prompted the peace negotiations. Three of the priests murdered had been my professors and mentors at the UCA. In 1992 the war ended and peace agreements were signed. My uncle Abelardo Torres, a former Salvadoran minister of the economy, was among the negotiators on the government's side.

After the war the people of Santa Marta crossed the wide and turbulent Lempa River and returned to El Salvador. At the time of my visit, some fifteen years after their return, they had prospered to the point where they had become a vanguard laboratory for the latest livestock, agricultural, and educational techniques, including a computer laboratory with satellite internet. Kristin Rosekrans, an educator with the Agency for International Development (AID), accompanied me in one of my trips and verified that the people of Santa Marta are still using Brazilian pedagogue Paulo Freire's popular education approach.[7]

The sixties in El Salvador and in most of Latin America were a remarkably exciting and visionary time that has not been replicated in recent history. Some called it a "new reformation," perhaps because since the sixteenth century the Church had not shown so much ebullience and change. Small Christian communities of workers, students, and peasants gathering to read the Bible in the light of the new theological currents multiplied all over the continent. The small-group church model has also proven very effective for conservative groups, as storefront evangelical churches have also multiplied to the point that now they constitute a real threat to the hegemony of the Roman Catholic Church.

Gustavo Gutiérrez

In December 1971, the Peruvian priest Gustavo Gutiérrez published his seminal work, *Teologia de la LIberación.*[8] In my opinion, the work has been unsurpassed in setting forth the main themes of liberation theology in a clear, methodical, and vigorous way. Gutiérrez's influential work was followed by a flurry of similar works by authors like Jon Sobrino[9] and Ignacio

5

Ellacuria[10] in El Salvador, Juan Luis Segundo in Uruguay,[11] Frei Betto[12] and Leonardo and Clodovis Boff[13] in Brazil, Pedro Trigo[14] and Otto Maduro[15] in Venezuela, Sergio Torres[16] and Pablo Richard[17] in Mexico, and José Miguez Bonino[18] and Enrique Dussel[19] in Argentina.

I met Father Gutiérrez during the summer of 1980 at the Theology of the Americas conference in Detroit. He is a very short man of predominantly native features. He limps because of having a shorter leg, and has to wear one high-heeled shoe to assist him in his balance. As soon as he began his presentation, however, we were all entranced. I had never heard such clear and well-substantiated exposition of liberation, or any other, theology. We rode together in a van afterward and he answered our questions clearly and concisely. It was a privilege and a delight to have been in the presence of this humble intellectual giant.

At the same conference I met Jesuit theologian Jon Sobrino, who was to become the only survivor of the Jesuit community massacre. Based on Gutiérrez's work, Sobrino developed the theoretical basis of liberation theology further by attempting to integrate Kant's philosophy into it. Sobrino analyzed the role ascribed to the use of reason as a valid and necessary tool to deal with the world of phenomena and develop a coherent ethical system. Later, Sobrino was to become one of the best advocates for Romero's canonization. More on this later.

Gutiérrez's main credit was the integration of Marxist analysis into theological thinking. In this manner, his theology attempted to achieve something similar to what Thomas

Aquinas did by assimilating Aristotle's philosophy into scholastic theology. Although one of the basic tenets of liberation theology is that it stems from the people at the bottom as an expression of their yearning, Gutiérrez's presentation clearly shows the influence of Marxist thought. Some called Gutiérrez's work the "Baptism of Marxism."

One of the main achievements of the Roman Catholic Church in Latin America was that it procured a first-rate education, in Europe or the United States, for some of its most promising clergy. In the 1960s Gutiérrez was sent to Belgium and France where he became acquainted with Marxist theory and with the Christian-Marxist dialogue taking place there. He did not, however, embrace the philosophical atheism of Marxist theory; he focused instead on the socioeconomic analysis of Marx's historical materialism. The new theology and historical materialism were, however, uneasy bedfellows.

Marx's depiction of class struggle and the conditions of the working class seemed totally suited to the realities Gutiérrez experienced in his native Peru and all over Latin America. The kind of individualism fostered by capitalism did not appear to him to be congruent with the Christian message. Instead, the collective vision of Marxism appealed to him, and other pastors, who were looking for a way out of oppressive conditions by promoting cooperatives, trade unions, and base communities.[20] Gutiérrez writes:

> Individualism operates, in fact, as a filter that makes it possible to "spiritualize" and even volatilize what in the Bible

are nuanced statements of a social and historical nature. For example, the poor/rich opposition (a social fact) is reduced to the humble/proud opposition (something within the individual). "Passage" through the individual interiorizes, and robs of their historical bite, categories reflective of the objective realities in which individuals and peoples live and die, struggle and assert their faith.[21]

Marxist analysis instead points to the actual conditions of the poor and offers a tool for concrete action.

> In a famous text Marx points out very precisely his contribution to the class struggle: not the discovery of its existence, but rather the analysis of its causes and an indication of the path to a classless society. The objective which Marx proposes is to abolish that which gives origin to the very existence of social classes. But the causes of the class struggle cannot be overcome without first becoming aware of the struggle and its demands in the process of building a new society.[22]

The favorite biblical text in Gutiérrez's work is the book of Exodus, which narrates the struggle of the Hebrew people to overcome the slavery to which they had been subjected in Egypt. It is worth noting that even after God delivered them from the yoke of Pharaoh the Israelites had to overcome the inner conditioning that propelled them to turn against Moses, their leader, and wish for a return to Egypt. People have to overcome both their outward and internalized oppression.

Historical materialism is the opposite of consumerist imperialism, which has become the norm in globalized society. Some, however, considered Marxism a Judeo-Christian heresy because it assumed that a special group of people, in this case the working-class proletariat, were free from the greed and foibles afflicting the whole of humanity. The subsequent failure of exclusively Marxist societies has greatly confirmed this assumption.

Gutiérrez's influence waned considerably since the nineties, partly because the liberation theology movement has suffered serious reversals because of both Vatican and American influence. Presently, in El Salvador the adherents of liberation theology constitute a remnant of what was a widespread popular movement. They meet every Sunday in the crypt of the Metropolitan Cathedral, where Romero is buried, whereas the people in general meet in the main nave upstairs. Toward the end of one his most recent articles Gutiérrez writes:

> The change begun at Medellin and ratified at Puebla gave
> many a new vision of the church in Latin America. . . . The
> challenges we face in Latin America are, of course, very
> great, and the changes needed are radical, even within the
> church. That is why Puebla several times called for the con-
> version of all Christians and of the church as a whole in face
> of the poverty prevalent throughout the region.[23]

Gutiérrez collaborated closely in the preparation of the conferences of Medellin and Puebla and served as a consultant to the Peruvian bishops. At those historic gatherings the prelates, who formerly had acted as feudal princes, began the process of turning into advocates for the poor and oppressed.

Medellin and Puebla

Prompted by the impetus given by the Second Vatican Council, which called for a restructuring of the Church to respond to the demands of the modern world, the Latin American Bishops Conference (CELAM) was able to establish a relative independence from the Vatican. The first memorable result was the historic 1968 meeting at Medellin, Colombia, where the Latin American Roman Catholic Church began to put forward the idea of a preferential option for the poor, calling for crucial and radical change and offering the concept of a God who championed for the poor and opposed the greed of the wealthy elites. It was a huge change for a church that for centuries had lived in alliance with the powerful. Russian Orthodox writer Fyodor Dostoyevsky said that the Roman Catholic Church had fallen prey to the third temptation of Jesus: worldly power. Curiously, in embracing liberation theology, it seemed as if the Church was trying to assert and maintain its power even in societies dominated by Marxist thought.

When the bishops began to realize that the ruling classes were poised to torture and kill not only lay leaders, but even priests and bishops who had previously been immune to such dangers, many began to doubt their former stances. A reaction promptly ensued. Within four years Archbishop (now Cardinal) Alfonso Lopez Trujillo, a hard-nosed, hard-driving executive, had regained control of CELAM, getting most of its agencies under his control. The mystique of Medellin, however, survived and thrived.

At Puebla, Mexico, where CELAM III was held in 1979, Lopez Trujillo's plans to create a backlash, although solidly backed by conservative prelates, achieved only an impasse. The final document was ambiguous in its repeated efforts to shift the focus from oppression (the Latin American reality) to secularization (the European reality). In fact, the Church worldwide was suffering from the effects of both, but nowhere so poignantly as in the Global South.

Puebla denounced the widespread and generalized poverty, which it correctly identified as systemic. But when it came to solutions, it ignored its own analysis, insisting instead that the problem was secularization, to be resolved by evangelization of the culture and not by a radical change of the social system. Evangelization of the culture has ever since been the slogan of the opponents of Medellin, although they have never clearly articulated it. The assault on Medellin has continued with little regard for either truth or kindness, thus confirming in practice the reality of ideological struggle, even within the church. Romero was not allowed to attend Puebla as an official representative of the episcopate, but only as an observer; he, however, was already seen as the icon of liberation theology, and was coveted by the media.

The objective of the Vatican Curia, with the support of Pope John Paul II, became to reverse Medellin and purge the Church from liberation theology and its preferential option for the poor. The pope, however, was also an advocate of human rights, though in a more critical and traditional way. According to an edict of Pope Paul VI, CELAM has no ultimate autonomy. CELAM was thus reduced to an advisory role. The pope in turn could disregard its recommendations or rewrite them, and could dismantle CELAM when he wished. As we shall see later, however, Paul VI was supportive of Romero when the conflict had reached a critical point.

I met Jean Paul II in Nicaragua, where I was stationed by the Episcopal Church's Volunteer for Mission. It was my first assignment after I was ordained. My wife was four months pregnant, but we walked about six miles to see him. The gigantic plaza was crowded with innumerable people, among whom were many protesters, wearing signs and chanting slogans. The pope began with just one word: "*Silencio* (Silence)"; and the entire multitude became instantly quiet. He was an impressive man. His sermon, delivered in perfect Spanish, was critical of liberation theology because of its emphasis on class struggle. He was a champion of Catholic orthodoxy; and even scolded the poet-priest and minister of culture Ernesto Cardenal, wagging his finger when the latter kneeled in front of him and asked for his blessing. The pontiff also criticized Ernesto's brother, who was a Jesuit priest and was the minister of education. The alleged reason was that priests should not serve in government. Father Robert Drinan, however, had served with no problem in the US House of Representatives; the real reason was that the government of Nicaragua had Marxist leanings.

Vatican II[24] elaborated on the concept of the "signs of the times" as historical indicators of divine will and, therefore, relevant to theology. As opposed to what liberation theology proposed, the conservative aim was to return to the former schemes where classical theology came first, then observation of the world, and finally the application of inherited theology to the world, instead of looking at historical reality first and then looking for guidance in theology and scripture.

The change, had it been successful, would have effectively eliminated liberation theology, a theology that is radically historical because it considers the liberation from oppressive structures; these are seen as the product, not of God's will, but of human greed, and as the pivotal problem of our present global reality. The change also promoted a different Christology, one no longer based on the historical Jesus but on the Christ of faith, as he was understood by prior generations and defined by the Church's councils. This, in fact, implies a hierarchical relationship of the people to God with the Church hierarchy as the mediator that dictates the rules, instead of discovering Christ in the actualized and lived, the love and service of neighbor.

Everything else followed. We are back in a world in which the way of salvation is strictly individual and ahistorical: receive the word, be converted, believe, be baptized, and receive forgiveness of sins and, later, the gift of the Spirit. It was a return to a superficially modernized version of the European, pre-Vatican II Church, which stressed a somewhat feudal scheme that was sacral, hierarchical, monarchical, canonical, and highly suspicious of the contemporary world.

The cosmetic modernization took the form of a theology of benevolence to replace the theology of liberation. A theology so defined denies the obvious fact of class struggle, insisting on a shared community of interests and objectives in society. According to liberation theologians, a moralistic response to injustice in social conditions has obviously failed to change the situation of oppression. In the conservative view, injustice is a problem affecting individuals, not groups or classes. Evangelical churches have used an individualistic approach to promote the cult of personal prosperity. Their approach has become an ally of consumerism, which is the secular religion of the twenty-first century.

According to this traditional view revived by the Vatican, what we need are charitable institutions contingent on the generosity of the wealthy. Justice then, according to conservative theologians, should be replaced by emphatic brotherly love. For liberation theologians this was a bogus solution; according to them most of the problems afflicting the poor have their origin in socioeconomic causes, which can only be overcome, not by the generosity of the rich, but by radical change in governments and institutions—that is, by systemic change.

Even after the advent of Francis, a Latin American pope, many in the Vatican continue to resent liberation theology as the product of third-world people who think they are entitled to participate in theological thinking, which has long been a European monopoly. In the final analysis, we have the confrontation of a conservative Church with its own gospel-based liberation identity. The challenge of liberation theology will persist as long as conditions of oppression continue to exist. The cry of Amos and all the prophets, of Romero and Martin Luther King, and of anyone who has become sensitized to actual suffering, are impossible to silence.

Romero was aware of the plight of the poor and wanted to help them in a charitable way. His contact, however, with the experience of repression and with liberation theology brought about a radical change in the way he went about responding to their needs.

Liberation Theology in Romero's Biographies

The thread of liberation theology is going to run through all of the works about Romero reviewed here and will inform this work also.

The first and, to date, most definitive biography of Romero was written by Jesuit priest James R. Brockman.[25] It was originally published as *The Word Remains* and revised by Brockman in 1989.

I called Father Brockman, the director of Hispanic ministry for the Catholic diocese in Little Rock, Arkansas, to request an interview and left a message. Two days later another Jesuit returned my call to let me know that he had passed away only a few days before. Thus, my attempts to follow up on his extensive research were tragically brought to a halt. However, his revised biography of Romero is carefully researched and contains a wealth of information that provided me with invaluable clues for my work.

The book does not follow a strict chronological order. It opens with the events from February to May 1977, describing the beginning of the persecution unleashed against the Roman Catholic clergy: the assassinations of Frs. Rutilio Grande and Alfonso Navarro, and Romero's reaction to those events, which spurned the beginning of his new ministry focused on structural social change. I met Alfonso Navarro when I was a student at San Jose Seminary in San Salvador and visited him at the parish where he was killed. In 2000 I returned to pay my respects at his grave, which is located in the same church. This first chapter details Romero's struggles to come to terms with the new liberation theology paradigm and with the overly pressing situation at hand precipitated by severe repression. We are walked through the decision-making process that led him to decree a controversial single Mass in the archdiocese on the Sunday following Father Grande's murder. It concludes with Romero's challenging the president, with whom he formerly had a friendly relationship, to respond to the atrocities.

For Brockman, what deserved most attention in Romero's existence was condensed into those years. This is a pattern we will see in all of his biographers. The pattern of dedicating more time to the ministry and achievements of the mature individual rather than to his childhood and formation is reminiscent of the gospel approach by which Jesus's story is also highly condensed into his last three years, with the rest of his life being such a blur that it is commonly referred to as "the hidden life" of Jesus of Nazareth.

Brockman narrates in detail Romero's confrontations with the other bishops and the papal nuncio. His work narrates the recrudescence of the persecution against the Church and the defamation campaign waged by the ruling class against the leftist clergy. Some of the most common epithets launched at the clergy were "Priests of Beelzebub, go back to Moscow," and "Shoemaker to your shoes." The implication was that the liberation theology-oriented clergy were meddling with matters outside their jurisdiction, which was supposed to be the salvation of individual souls.

Also, they were portrayed as agents of an international communist conspiracy. The most formidable opponent Romero came across in this period was Cardinal Mario Casariego from Guatemala. He was a conservative Spanish priest loyal to the government who had worked in El Salvador where he ran an orphanage. At that institution, children were subjected to cruel corporal punishment. Casariego began, at that time, to wage a systematic campaign against the progressive clergy in El Salvador. The press seized on Casariego's pronouncements to attack the progressive clergy and reinforce the perception of them as subversives, rogue priests, and, basically, fair game for the army and the death squads.

The period of Romero's second pastoral letter, in which he spells out his understanding of the Church's role in society, also gets considerable attention in this work. It delves into Romero's understanding of the Church as Christ incarnated in the suffering people. It details also his difficulties with a rebel priest named Antonio Quinteros, who contributed to the defamation campaign against him, feeding stories to the press about Romero being the leader of a guerrilla organization. It also details his mounting difficulties with the papal nuncio, Monsignor Gerada, and his personal confrontation with him, which marked the onset of his alienation from highly placed sources in the Vatican and the beginnings of a friendly relationship with the progressive Jesuits.

Brockman also relates the events of January to June 1978, beginning with Romero's reception of the honorary degree conferred to him by Georgetown University, followed by the vicissitudes of his relationship with the rest of the episcopate, particularly Bishop Aparicio from San Vicente, leading to the closing in of a circle of hostility between Romero and the conservative factions in church and state, and Romero's continued denunciation of governmental injustices. It also details his trip to Rome and his fortuitous meeting with Pope Paul VI, also canonized on the same date as Romero, who told him *coraggio* (Italian): meaning, have courage, you are in charge!

Romero's third pastoral letter is dedicated to delineating the relationship of the Church to the popular organizations; the role of violence is also detailed. It is here that Romero mapped out his most controversial teaching, which took the traditional doctrine of just war to its most radical logical conclusion, which is revolutionary violence. Formerly this concept had been applied to mutual hostilities between duly constituted governments, now it was being applied to the right to insurrection by disaffected sectors of the population. It continues to detail his difficulties with the hierarchy and government and the ups and downs of his relationship to Monsignor Revelo, a longtime associate who turned vehemently against him. It also describes the crisis set off by the death of Father Ernesto Barrera, a priest who allegedly died in a shooting match with government troops and who was an active member of a popular organization. Ernesto was a classmate and friend of mine at San Jose Seminary.

The events from July to December 1978 singled out by Brockman include the assassination of Father Octavio Ortiz, who worked with poor marginal communities in the outskirts of San Salvador, and the wave of protests occasioned by the same. I met Octavio when we were both students at San Jose Seminary. Romero's continued difficulties with the government of now President Arturo Romero (not a relative), prompted the people to say that it was a fight between the two Romeros and to wonder which one of them would win. My uncle, General Fidel Torres, who was minister of defense under President Sanchez Hernandez, pointed out to me that General Romero was the last in a long line of military presidents in El Salvador.

The rise of the Popular Revolutionary Block (BPR) and of other popular organizations and the buildup toward an armed insurgency movement are also described. The Latin American bishops' conference in Puebla, Mexico, took place in this period. Romero's role in that conference, though not official, was very influential. At that event the media gravitated toward him rather than to the conservative prelates.

June to October 1979 witnessed the escalating violence on both sides, but mostly the governmental brutality and the widespread use of torture. Another priest from the archdiocese, Rafael Palacios, was killed in this period. Romero's documented alienation from the rest of the hierarchy continued to escalate and he became established as the main human rights advocate in El Salvador.

In October 13, 1979, a cadre of progressive military officers and civilians engineered a coup d'etat and took power with the stated intention to institute crucial reforms. Romero's response to the coup d'etat was one of cautious support. It was the first time in fifty years that a coalition of civilians and military ruled in El Salvador. The junta was short lived because it failed to deliver its promise to control the military. Human rights violations continued unabated and the civilians in the junta resigned to dissociate themselves from the carnage. The junta was succeeded by a Christian democratic government that experienced the same fate. Brockman depicts Romero's struggle to maintain his support for the junta, which he regarded as a possible peaceful solution, in spite of his close associates' warnings against his supporting it.

The most dramatic portion of the book covers the events from February to March 1980 and details the crescendo of violence and confrontation, culminating with Romero's last Sunday homily in which he impugned the military to stop the killing and repression, and the soldiers to disobey their military superiors. This was tantamount to a declaration of war. Allegedly, this led to his assassination on March 24, 1980, although it is likely that plans for the crime had started long ago.

There is an appendix on Romero's killers, which describes the pretense of an investigation into his death, the abuses of power, and the flaws in the Salvadoran legal system, which aborted the investigation and proceedings. We also have a glimpse here of the men suspected of this most heinous crime, particularly Roberto D'Aubuisson, who was broadly believed to be the person responsible for planning and ordering Romero's execution. I met D'Aubuisson's sister Marisa on several occasions, once unexpectedly at a luncheon at the beach home of a friend of mine, Miguel Gallardo, who was also her cousin; years later, Miguel was killed at gunpoint in a restaurant, his murder was never investigated. Marisa is a former nun of upper-middle-class extraction who left her order because it was preventing her from working with the poor. Subsequently she married an ex-Roman Catholic priest. She attends the Masses in memory of Monsignor Romero every Sunday at San Salvador's Metropolitan Cathedral, and was always an opponent of her brother's ideology and tactics.

Brockman's opus makes for a most fascinating historical and theological reading. His writing is easy to follow and the book almost reads like a novel, or should I say a gospel, as he delves into the web of events that culminated in Romero's martyrdom. From all of the extant biographies, his is the one that gives us more of a glimpse into the archbishop's complex personality. Although relatively little space is dedicated to Romero's inner life in the book as a whole, his work was very helpful in pointing me in the right direction because of the abundance of historical detail about the character's last and decisive three years and the information about his acquaintances. It is through Brockman that I learned the role Mr. Salvador Barraza played, as Romero's closest friend. Liberation theology plays a major role, according to Brockman, in Romero's change.

The second comprehensive biography to be published was written by Jesús Delgado, a Salvadoran diocesan priest who held the honorific title of Monsignor (not a bishop).[26] He was the former dean of the Metropolitan Cathedral in San Salvador. Subsequently he was accused of sexual misconduct with his female domestic employee; which, given the strictness of the celibacy rule, is not a rare accusation among the Catholic clergy in El Salvador. Delgado, however, fell into disgrace after this. To my knowledge his book has not yet been translated into English.

Thanks to the good offices of Mr. Salvador Barraza, Father Delgado, reluctantly, granted me a brief interview at the diocesan headquarters in San Salvador. He seemed annoyed by my request to use a tape recorder. Perhaps the fact that I ended up using it after he grudgingly accepted influenced the rest of the conversation. He answered my questions in a curt and matter-of-fact way; basically, he stonewalled me, and I was unable to gather any significant new information. Romero was a saint and that was it.

Delgado briefly covers Romero's childhood, his seminary formation, his time as a student in Rome, his return to El Salvador, and his early ministry in the provincial capital of San Miguel. This is the most personal section of the work.

A lot of the work is dedicated to his so called "conversion"[27] years, since he was transferred to San Salvador to be the secretary of the Salvadoran Bishops Conference, his Episcopal consecration and service first as auxiliary bishop of San Salvador and then as bishop of the Diocese of Santiago de Maria, where, according to the Spanish Passionist missionaries who served in that diocese, he began to move in the direction of social change and liberation theology.

The events of 1977 when Romero's closest friend and twin soul, Jesuit father Rutilio Grande, was assassinated are contemplated in more detail. Delgado traces the events leading to the tragedy. His book also explores the role of this tragedy in the course of subsequent events, for example, the momentous single Mass held in San Salvador to protest the government's passivity in investigating the crimes and abuses, and the participation of the armed forces in their commission.

The major portion of the work covers only three years, the ones that elapsed between Grande's and Romero's deaths. These were the years leading to a formal declaration of war between the guerrillas and the army in which the Church played a pivotal role. They depict kidnappings, the rise of popular movements, massive protests, and other demonstrations of popular unrest. They include theological and theoretical reflection about Marxism and Christianity and the role of the Church in the modern world. A lot of attention is focused on the Church's doctrinal changes originating in the Second Vatican Council and reinforced at the Latin American bishops' conference in Medellin, Colombia. Very little can be discerned about

Romero's personality from Delgado's depiction of Romero. The work is mostly a eulogy about how serene, courageous, and noble he was in the face of overwhelming odds.

Delgado's book follows the pattern of Brockman's and subsequent biographies. The man becomes secondary to the theological, social, and political considerations that were being woven around him. Like Brockman, more space is dedicated to the years in which social and political events become more turbulent. It is as if Romero's flesh and blood personality was accidental to the grander divine historical design in which he was immersed. However, perhaps unwittingly, the book does capture some of the veneer and the atmosphere of growing up in El Salvador. This is undoubtedly due to the author's own nationality and shared culture. The chapter on Romero's childhood is more picturesque and charming, though less informative than Brockman's.

Jon Sobrino's[28] biography is the most theologically oriented. The first part is supposedly dedicated to some personal reminiscences of the author's personal encounters with Romero but even this is interspersed with theological reflections and colored by the author's profound admiration for the archbishop. Sobrino is a Jesuit priest and the only survivor of the massacre where all of his colleagues were dragged out of their residence at the Catholic University (UCA), located in the northern part of San Salvador, and shot at close range in the head on November 16, 1989. Only Sobrino was spared because he was traveling overseas. Three of the other priests assassinated, Ignacio Martin Baro, Segundo Montes, and

Ignacio Ellacuria, were my professors at the same institution where I studied for two years, (1971 to 1973) before transferring to Baldwin Wallace College in Berea, Ohio. Sobrino has been singled out as one of the Jesuits who helped Romero prepare his explosive homilies, and possibly influenced him. The latter was *vox populi* (common knowledge), but I was not able to corroborate this, possibly because of the delicate matter of this assertion and the stonewalling that went with it.

I approached Father Sobrino for an interview but my petition was denied. He told me he was overwhelmed with requests and that he had recently granted an interview to a German author whose name he did not disclose. The fact that I was a Salvadoran writing about Romero and that this is to be the first psychobiography was not helpful in this case. However, he led me to his book on Romero, which, he said, contained some of his personal impressions on the archbishop.

Throughout the first and only more or less biographical chapter of his book, Sobrino strives to disprove the accusation that Romero was brainwashed by the Jesuits and manipulated to become their liberation theology champion. In my opinion his effort is persuasive but not fully convincing. Jon Sobrino was singled out as the main author of the first drafts of the archbishop's pastoral letters, which then Romero reviewed and changed only slightly. Sobrino's work does, however, briefly acknowledge the psychological ailments that characterized Romero and made his ministry difficult as his periods of depression interfered with the continuity of his work and his relations with coworkers. He also notes the humble origins of

the future prelate. But, all in all, Sobrino's work is an elaborate theological work that explores the religious, prophetic, and evangelical dimensions of Romero's ministry. These theological aspects are also relevant in a psychobiography dealing with a religious figure.

Maria Lopez Vigil's *Piezas Para un Retrato* (Memories in a Mosaic),[29] is the most charming and picturesque of all the biographical works. She is a committed journalist who admires Romero and dedicated her book to the Salvadoran people. The work is based on a series of interviews, which collect stories, anecdotes, incidents, and jokes on the life of the archbishop. The book is divided into two sections. The first, which is one third of the biography, deals with Romero's early years and the second, twice as long, deals with his ministry as an archbishop, which took place only in the last three years of his life. The sections are divided into episodes named after the more characteristic feature of the story or anecdote narrated by one or more of the persons interviewed. Thus, the first episode is called "Shepherd of Sheep and Wolves" and depicts Romero's ministry to both rich and poor in Santiago de Maria; the second, "A Little Inquisitor," describes an episode in Romero's early years in San Salvador and his fastidious watch over the more progressive elements in the diocese.

The book is very instructive in revealing Romero's sense of humor and his colloquial, sometimes peasant-like, use of language. The work does not follow a strict chronological order but the author does manage to interview a great many of the people who had some significant personal contact with him.

One of the work's setbacks is that the people being interviewed are not properly identified, only named; we are not told who they are or their relationship to Romero. One has to be familiar with the cast of characters surrounding the archbishop either from personal knowledge or from other works. Sometimes one is able to glean their identity from the stories but this is not always the case.

The anecdotes, although they may be embellished by the witnesses' own recollection and sense of humor, do manage to capture some of Romero's own trajectory and style. For the purposes of this work the accounts may be most helpful in terms of collecting other people's impressions about him, which come to form a mosaic, as the translator calls it; this becomes instrumental in completing our own puzzle image.

A shorter biographical work is that of Father Placido Erdozain.[30] I met Father Placido when he was a parish priest in San Salvador and I was a member of the Christian Student Movement. I encountered him again in Nicaragua, where I was stationed from 1982 to 1984 as a missioner from the Episcopal Church and subsequently as a mental health worker, and collaborated with him in providing pastoral care to the Salvadoran refugee communities there. He was a pious and faithful priest who upheld the right of the armed opposition to have chaplains: in other words, not to become enlisted, but to minister to the combatants. He was fond of using a phrase that captures a great deal of the liberation theology mystique that characterized Romero's approach: "to accompany the people in their struggle."

27

Erdozain's book is a much shorter work and deals exclusively with Romero's ministry as an archbishop, roughly from 1977 to 1980. Like the other religiously inspired biographies it is mostly a historical, theological, and sociological analysis of Romero's ministry and fails to add much of substance to the rest. Basically, it adds another volume to the abundant hagiographical material. It is notable, however, as a concise compilation of the most relevant historical facts surrounding the prelate's last and most controversial years and it can be very useful as far as those data are concerned.

Salvador Carranza Oña's *Romero—Rutilio: Vidas Encontradas*[31] is also a short treatise that purports to examine the relationship between the two men. Unfortunately, only the first twenty-three pages are dedicated to the subject the book purports to deliver. The first section describes Romero's ministry. The rest of the work consists of a compilation of Rutilio's sermons and devotional writings.

I was unable to find anything new or revealing in those twenty-three pages dealing with Romero and Rutilio's relationship, or to develop any new insights from it. The book is mainly descriptive of the pastoral work and ministry they carried out separately or together while they shared a friendship, with a brief look at Rutilio's funeral and Romero's reaction to his death, which has been singled out as the catalyst of Romero's change. All in all, I was able to find more detail about their relationship in Brockman and in an anonymous work about the life of Rutilio quoted elsewhere that delves deeply into the personality affinities that brought the two men together.

Ways of Seeing Romero

Zacarias Diez and Juan Macho's *En Santiago de Maria Me Tope con La Miseria*[32] covers in a rather extensive way the scarcely two years Romero spent as bishop of the Diocese of Santiago de Maria in the eastern part of El Salvador. The main hypothesis of this work is that it was while serving in that location that Romero changed into an advocate of structural social change. The authors contend that they were largely responsible for Romero's conciousness raising and teaching him liberation theology. They also claim that this happened when Romero had to deal with two major incidents, the first relating to the conflict over a peasant training and consciousness-raising center, which was perceived as indoctrination, and the second, a massacre carried out by the National Guard against the local peasants.

The authors are two Spanish priests belonging to the Passionist religious order. These two priests covered a rural parish of fifty thousand severely impoverished people and were among the first to implement the socially oriented pastoral directives of the Medellin Latin American bishops' conference.

The book is divided into six parts. The first deals with the background of the diocese and the authors' parish in social, ecclesial, and religious terms. It also includes a description of the *campesino* (peasant farmer) training center called "Los Naranjos (The Orange Trees)," which became a bone of contention because of the liberation theology being taught there and the involvement of a priest from another diocese. The Orange Trees became a headache for Romero, who felt compelled to conciliate the traditionalists with the radicals.

The work describes his less than triumphal entry into his new place of work in December 1974 and the expectations and reservations of the people who received him. It also gives a profile of the social and theological ideas of Romero at that time. It also details the massacre at the hamlet of Tres Calles, the case of Los Naranjos center, the extradition and subsequent reintegration of Father Juan Macho, and Romero's responses to those events.

This biography is peppered with a series of anecdotes and stories illustrating the future martyr's interest in serving and listening to the poor. In addition, it describes the pastoral organization in the diocese, which made use of lay people as pastoral agents, and the increasing social projection of the diocesan work.

The work contains the authors' reminiscences about Romero. At this point they seem to have forgotten about the stormy and problematic relationship they had with him. In my opinion, the chapter projects backward the profound change, virtues, and achievements that the authors observed after Romero became archbishop.

The book does give evidence, in the forms of correspondence and vividly told stories, about the way in which Romero, by witnessing repression, softened to the plight of the poor. The authors suggest that his confrontation with escalating violence in that location somewhat prepared him for the increased persecution against the Church that awaited him in San Salvador.

In the end the work is valuable in documenting the eve of Romero's transformation in the two years that preceded his elevation to the archiepiscopal office and the beginning of his experience of the ways in which liberation theology was affecting people's lives.

I will draw extensively on the above-mentioned biographies as secondary sources in reconstructing the texture of Romero's emotional life, his historical context, and the role played by liberation theology and its adherents in Romero's remarkable transformation.

A question may be raised about the eschatology of liberation theology, that is, its failure to bring about a new society. The same can be said of Marxism or Christianity. A more valid inquiry would be whether liberation theology approximates the Christian ideal in a more effective way than traditional theologies do, but that would have to be the subject of another paper, and a monumental one at that.

CHAPTER 2
CHILDHOOD AND YOUTH

Growing up in El Salvador (1917–1930)

Oscar Arnulfo Romero y Galdamez was born on August 15, 1917, in a small village called Ciudad Barrios located in the province of San Miguel in the northeastern part of El Salvador. The indigenous name for the town was Cacahuatique, because the valuable cocoa plant (cacao) grew abundantly in the region. Despite the name of the town, by the time Romero was born the main crop in the region was coffee. The name Ciudad Barrios derives from President Gerardo Barrios, who promoted the cultivation of coffee as the main cash crop for exportation, thus stunting the diversification of the economy and creating a ruthless coffee baron oligarchy.

The introduction of coffee as the single export crop became a curse for El Salvador. Sociologist Liisa North writes,

El Salvador became a coffee export economy, a country whose patterns of economic growth and stagnation were to

33

be fundamentally determined by the character and performance of the export sector. Its economic well-being derived directly from how much coffee was produced and sold, and at what prices. In addition to the dangers inherent in dependence on a single crop, the extreme concentration of land and income within the coffee oligarchy prohibited the development of a strong domestic market. The coffee producers became "luxury importers" while most of the population was denied sufficient income to become consumers of domestically produced agricultural and industrial goods. The wages of agricultural workers in the coffee sector were low even by Third World standards.[1]

Greed and bribery by the big landowners and corruption among governmental officials gradually took away the lands of the indigenous people and the small landowners, a process that had a strong impact in the eventual impoverishment of the Romero family.

I visited Ciudad Barrios with Salvador Barraza and saw the house that stands where the Romero's house used to be. The building houses a farmers' cooperative association. It is located in a corner of the main plaza diametrically opposite to the town's church located in the other corner. The present church is newer but retains the ancient charm and beauty of colonial style religious architecture, which consists of many niches and naves, with dark and enveloping spaces that gave them a womb-like feeling. The church Oscar knew as a child was also built in the colonial style, which may have exerted a peculiar fascination in the little boy who demonstrated a special attachment to his mother and a great attraction to things religious.

Oscar's parents, Santos Romero and Guadalupe de Jesús Galdamez, were small landowners. Santos also worked as a telegrapher and postmaster. Little Oscar assisted his father in delivering telegraphs around town. His father was a cultured man who taught young Oscar to read music and play the flute. Subsequently, Oscar learned to play the piano and harmonium, which later became a source of solace and relaxation for the archbishop. Several friends of his told me that after a particularly difficult day Romero unwound by playing some of his favorite pieces of music.

Land tenure had determined social status in El Salvador since 1870, when the foundations of an agrarian republic were established. By those standards we may categorize the Romero family in Oscar's early years as modestly well off, though they did not have electricity, which was the lot of the majority of the people at the time.

The location of their home in Ciudad Barrios attests to the fact that they possessed some means, because living close to the center of town was a sign of higher social status. His brother Gaspar, a warm and open man who received us in his home located in a lower-middle-class neighborhood in San Salvador, denied that the indigent beginnings of the future archbishop predisposed him against the rich. He called that assertion an ill-intentioned myth, presumably invented by the left to suggest Romero was angry at their family's lot. Conversely, his younger brother Mamerto assured me that early economic hardship played a major role in the future archbishop's attitude toward the rich. But, without a doubt, in spite of Gaspar and Mamerto's disagreement, we do know that the relatively comfortable beginnings of the Romero family gave way to hard times, as the result of a wicked man's swindle, and this was likely to have had some influence in the future martyr's response to exploitation.

Romero's anger as a factor in his ministry leads us to the question of the dividing line between righteous indignation versus ordinary human wrath. That question could be the subject of a whole encyclopedia; however, we will attempt to discern some answers in this work. As the coffee fever exacerbated the desire of the oligarchy to expand their holdings, they gradually dispossessed most of the smaller landowners in El Salvador, including the Romeros. In 1932, the worldwide depression struck Salvadorans particularly hard; thousands of hungry peasants rose up in arms crying out for land. The rebellion was brutally repressed by a psychopathic dictator, General Maximiliano Hernandez Martinez, who shot and hanged over thirty thousand peasants in the first week of the conflict. This peculiar president, who professed to be a theosophist,[2] believed in esoteric remedies and held eccentric beliefs. For example, during a severe epidemic of cholera he surrounded the city of San Salvador with multicolored lights in order to stop the disease. He believed that it was worse to kill an ant than a human being because the former had fewer opportunities to reincarnate as a human being. Martinez's brutality in crushing the rebellion is typical of the succession of military dictatorships who ruled El Salvador for most of the twentieth century, including in Romero's time.

Romero was fifteen years old when the revolt began. At that time, he was still in minor seminary, the equivalent of high school with religious discipline and instruction. The massacre began in the western part of El Salvador where most of the surviving indigenous communities were located. The native Pipiles were distant relatives of the Tlaxcaltecs, an indigenous Mexican tribe who fought with Spanish conquistador Hernan Cortes against the Aztecs and brought the Nahuat language to some parts of Central America, including El Salvador.[3] Like the Mayans in Guatemala today, they resisted their integration into *Ladino*, or Westernized society.

Although some Ladinos saw themselves as white, because of the racial mixture in the country they also had native blood, for the most part. Prompted mostly by the prevailing and worsening conditions of hunger in the countryside, the peasants responded to the agitation carried out by militants of the Communist Party of El Salvador, although such influence has been greatly exaggerated. The leader of the incipient communist movement was Farabundo Marti—hence the name of the alliance of guerrilla forces during the 1980s civil war: Frente Farabundo Marti de Liberacion Nacional (Farabundo Marti National Liberation Front). It was also the name of the leftist party founded by the guerrillas who ruled for two terms and then lost in a landslide because of internal corruption and demagoguery.

The rebellion did not happen overnight; it was the outcome of a century of gradual peasant dispossession. The peasants fought using machetes, sticks, and a few outdated rifles. It is estimated that overall, the rebels killed a couple of hundred policemen and soldiers. The toll of the ensuing army repression has been estimated at thirty thousand.[4] Thomas Anderson relates the terror in Izalco, one of the main indigenous villages:

> As most of the rebels, except the leaders, were difficult to identify, arbitrary classifications were set up. All those who were carrying machetes were considered guilty. All those dressed in a scruffy, *campesino* costume were also considered guilty. To facilitate the roundup all those who had not taken part in the uprising were invited to present themselves to the *comandancia* (military command post), to receive clearance papers. When they arrived, they were examined and those with the above-mentioned attributes seized. Tied by the thumbs to those before and behind them, in the customary Salvadoran manner, groups of fifty were led to the back wall of the church of Asuncion in Izalco and against the massive wall were cut down by the firing squads. In the plaza in front of the *comandancia* other selected victims were made to dig a mass grave and then shot, according to one account, from machine guns mounted on trucks. In some cases, women and children refused to leave their menfolk and shared their fate. An old Izalco resident who was then a soldier in the army, says there is no doubt that the *guardia* behaved much worse than the rebels, "shooting anyone they came across."[5]

I will revisit this event when I deal with the roots of the 1980s civil war in El Salvador.

It is important to note the nefarious role racism has played in El Salvador. The native populations have been consistently kept at the bottom of the social ladder, whereas people of European descent hold privilege and are treated with special consideration. This internalized racism is known as *malinchismo,* after Malinche, the native Mexican woman who became the lover of Spanish conqueror Hernan Cortes. During the massacre that followed the 1932 peasant insurrection, the lesser number of light-skinned *Mestizos* or *Ladinos* (people of mixed descent) were shot, whereas the natives were hanged—a more economic and painful form of killing. It would be hard to believe that the insurrection did not make a strong impression on the young Romero's sensitive personality.

I was born fourteen years after the *Matanza* and still I was shaken by the accounts of the massacre from my maternal grandfather, who was predominantly of indigenous descent. It is important to note that there must have been a racial solidarity in Romero, who was also Mestizo, with the lot of the indigenous people. This was certainly the case with some members of my family who, though very light skinned, were still aware of their indigenous roots. It has certainly been the case with me, as I have struggled all my life with the spurious denial of the racism prevalent in El Salvador. The Romeros owned a moderate amount of land and were light-skinned Mestizos, which accounted for a complex sense of identity in the life of young

Oscar. In spite of any attenuations or ambiguities, in the end the Romeros went the way of their unfortunate native ancestors.

Contrary to the wishes of his father, Oscar did not pursue a secular occupation. His father wanted him to be a carpenter. But young Oscar was closer to his mother, particularly in terms of her dedication to the Catholic Church and faith. All accounts seem to indicate that; Romero used to play saying Mass and organizing processions in the honor of the Blessed Virgin Mary as a young boy. His surviving sister, Zaida, a lovely octogenarian, described to me the devotion with which he would lead these mock processions. However, in spite of the fact that most churchgoing people were, and still are, women, he adamantly excluded girls from these activities. It was strictly a boy's game. One interesting detail related by Zaida is that little Oscar used to put on one of mother's aprons and go around on the streets calling out to the other kids pretending he was already a priest.[6]

It is not hard to imagine how a little boy wearing a woman's apron would be treated in a predominantly macho culture. The metaphor of the mother for the Church is a powerful one. It was a natural outlet and refuge for the boy's disposition toward his natural mother, as well as a further sign of his inclinations. Zaida also said, "As a boy he seemed a little sad. My brother always turned inward, thought too much."[7]

Then there is the mystery surrounding a childhood illness that prevented him from joining in rougher boys' games and contributed to his reclusive personality. Some said it was *mal de ojo* (the evil eye), an unspecified illness brought about by a sorcerer or a person with negative vibrations; this is the stuff of the folklore culture Romero was born into. The tradition was already widespread in Europe and was imported to Latin America. According to *The Skeptic's Dictionary*, "The evil eye is a kind of curse put on a child, livestock, crops, etc., by someone who has the 'evil eye.'" There does not seem to be any particular reason why some people are born with and others without the evil eye. The curse is usually unintentional and caused by praising and looking enviously at the victim. In Sicily and southern Italy, however, it is believed that some people— *jettatore*[8]—are malevolent and deliberately cast the evil eye on their victims. Belief in the evil eye is not necessarily associated with witchcraft or sorcery, though the evil eye was something Church inquisitors were instructed to look for. Pope Pius IX was reputed to be a *jettatore*, not because he was thought to be malevolent but rather because it seemed that disasters fell upon persons and places he had blessed. I was unable to find out specifically what Romero's illness was all about.

Santos Romero was not a religious man. He had to be given religious instruction before marriage, which suggests that he lacked knowledge of the foundations of the Catholic faith. He had young Oscar memorize the basic prayers, however, as he later recalled in a lament about the death of his father. Santos also used strict corporal punishment. According to Mamerto, the younger brother, he used to have the boys kneel for a long time on grains of corn to atone for their mischievousness, and he even fell asleep and forgot about them when he did so. Amazingly, in spite of suffering this rather cruel form of punishment, Mamerto remembers Oscar getting up in the middle of the night to kneel and pray. Perhaps this was a kind of masochistic expiation on the part of the overly conscientious boy for real or fantasized offenses against the earthly or heavenly father.

What offense could have been so heinous, for Oscar to believe it was justified to be punished and to punish himself further? He was a pubescent boy, so it was normal and plausible that he masturbated, which might have generated a great deal of guilt in him, giving rise to the need to expiate in a way that was familiar and prescribed. The conflicts over sexuality and the kneeling behavior started early in Romero's life and continued well into adulthood. It was rumored that Romero, during his early years as a priest, listened to the pope's (the Holy Father's) recorded allocutions every day on his knees so he that he could later apply the pope's teachings to his own pastoral endeavors.[9]

The local clergy, through the good offices of the town mayor, who had become aware of the boy's devotion, soon discovered Oscar's inclinations and recruited him for the minor seminary, the equivalent of a high school that also included early and extensive religious instruction. The seminary was located in the provincial capital of San Miguel. Because of the piety, intelligence, and intense dedication Romero showed in minor seminary, he was singled out as a promising candidate to rise within the Catholic hierarchy. When Oscar was offered a chance to attend the Gregorian University in Rome, his family was forced to mortgage the best portion of their lands to finance his higher education, since the Church would only provide for part of the expenses. Unfortunately, the land fell into the hands of a speculator who managed, by dubious legal means, to despoil the Romeros from their properties, and they soon found themselves indigent. His brother Arnoldo, who still lives in San Miguel, described to me how his mother, already a widow, pitifully begged the swindler for an opportunity to redeem their lands, and how the speculator cold-heartedly refused.

Riches to Rags (1936–1944)

Gaspar Romero related to me how his family became dispossessed. Several family members reported that in 1936, while Oscar was still in Rome studying for the priesthood, Santos fell deeply into alcoholism and died from alcohol withdrawal, probably delirium tremens.[10] I was unable to determine how old he was when he died. When he was already very ill, he entrusted his properties to a man named Claudio Portillo, who was the godfather of Arnoldo, one of Oscar younger brothers, with the condition that he would administer the patrimony and look out for the family. According to Gaspar, the godfather was a thief and a murderer. He owned several saloons in Ciudad Barrios where he got the customers drunk and robbed them. Sometimes he gave orders for angry customers to be beaten up and some died from the severity of the beatings. Gaspar did not remember exactly when Santos fell prey to alcoholism, but he said it was customary for the mayor, the judge, and the telegraph operator to get together and drink heavily, a kind of pastime and bonding, which is how Oscar's father's disease became lethal.

Gaspar was only seven when his father passed away, and Oscar was nineteen. It takes approximately ten years of heavy drinking to develop delirium, so it seems likely that Santos Romero suffered from alcoholism when Romero was a little boy, which offers another reason Oscar gravitated so much toward his mother. I verified with Gaspar that Santos did not drink as a result of the loss of his estate but rather that his illness led to the family's downfall by his error of judgment in entrusting his family's future to a wicked man. In Gaspar's words, "He (the speculator) amassed his fortune at the expense of many tears."[11]

Alcoholism ran in the family. The eldest surviving brother, Gustavo Romero, also died from the disease, and even Gaspar confessed to having had periods of heavy drinking. At any rate, alcoholism has always been endemic in El Salvador, a country besieged by multiple and severe socioeconomic pressures. The father's alcoholism is likely to have had a profound effect in the life of the future martyr. The lack of a consistent father figure most likely contributed to the child's insecurity and lack of assertiveness, or to inappropriate expression of anger, often turned against himself.[12]

The truth of the matter seems to be that a combination of factors led to the family's downfall. On the one hand, Oscar's education necessitated mortgaging their property, which might have been handled well if Santos had been in possession of his faculties, but they were atrophied by alcoholism. Arnoldo Romero told me that Oscar, who because of his position as a member of the clergy had become the family's oracle, persuaded them to desist from litigating after they were despoiled from their lands. At the time, Romero's family vehemently loathed his conformity and smoothing over troubles. Later, this demureness was ascribed to the saintly character of the martyred archbishop, although, perhaps, it was also a deficiency of assertiveness and healthy aggression in his personality.

Many years later the Romeros recovered their patrimony. Gaspar said the Romero children labored under the strain of severe hardship doing menial agricultural work to earn the equivalent of ten dollars a month for many years. The impact of the fraud was so profound on Romero's mother that she suffered a stroke and half of her body became paralyzed. Gaspar said his mother did the household chores like cooking and washing using only her right hand.

Later, Gaspar was able to obtain a job as a telegraph and post office delivery boy. After that he graduated to telegraph operator and obtained a position in the capital city of San Salvador. When he was twenty-three, he returned to Ciudad Barrios because he was a friend of the town's mayor. At that time, he learned the whole shocking truth that not only had they been dispossessed from the original coffee farm but also other parcels of land belonging to them. Even the house they used to live in had been misappropriated by Mr. Portillo, who had accepted their inheritance in the name of the family. He and the mayor had a few drinks of strong Salvadoran liquor called *espiritu de caña* (spirit of sugarcane) and they decided to pay Mr. Portillo a visit. Gaspar confronted him with the crime and told him he had to make restitution immediately. The old man adamantly refused, alleging that he would arrange matters with Oscar when he returned from Rome; he knew Oscar was easier to manipulate. Gaspar insisted that he arrange matters with him immediately. When the old man stubbornly refused, Gaspar pulled out a gun from his belt and said, "You will arrange matters with me or you will die you son of a whore!"

The mayor counseled Portillo to comply, saying, "This man is angry and he is drunk and he will surely kill you." The mayor then pulled out a manual typewriter that he was conveniently carrying and typed a legal deed that stated that the swindler sold the properties to Gaspar for "x" amount of money as a way to simplify matters, since trying to recover the lands as inheritance was complicated by the fact that there were several children alive, which meant it could get tangled up in legal hurdles. Gaspar, being a master storyteller, embellished the tale with more or less accurate details; my conversations with the other relatives, however, confirmed that the land had indeed been recovered.

After receiving the properties, Gaspar redistributed them to all brothers and gave the house to the only sister, Zaida. She had married at fifteen and was recently divorced and destitute. When the son of Mr. Portillo found out how his father had been forced to return the properties, he pulled out his own gun and went looking for Gaspar. First, he went to city hall looking for the mayor who told him it was too late. The properties had already been registered and it was already official. Gaspar was nowhere to be found.

Whereas Gaspar was aggressive, gregarious, and decisive, those close to Oscar described him as anxious and unable to develop camaraderie and friendship. He was also passive, withdrawn, and averse to socializing. Everyone I interviewed attested to his perfectionism, even as a young man. His ailment has been commonly recognized among the clergy as the disease of *scruples*,[13] which is characterized by indecisiveness and a need to keep everything tidy, including one's beliefs and doctrine. In psychiatric jargon, we might label it as obsessive-compulsive disorder. To name the affliction is not to detract from Romero, but to bear witness to the fact that Grace can and does act even through persons plagued by psychological ailments; the germs of mental instability should make any purported divine intervention even more relevant and become a cause for hope.

The pattern of Holy Scripture tells us that God chooses the most unlikely characters to carry out God's plan of salvation. Think of Peter, Paul, and the first disciples. The same can be said of Ezekiel, Job, King David, Augustine of Hippo, and Francis of Assisi. In fact, perhaps with the exception of Jesus of Nazareth, it becomes hard to find a single holy person or prophet who is not shaped by more than their fair share of human blemishes and failings. The Bible seems to hammer this in order to drive home the point that salvation is a gift from above.

Erik Erikson's masterly case study of young Martin Luther documented how Luther underwent debilitating periods of depression and, alternately, was so energized that he was able to write immense theological treatises—what we might label as bipolar disorder today. Sometimes Luther became so delusional that he threw inkpots at the devil. A similar coexistence of pathology and saintliness could well also prove to be the case with Romero, which may be one of the reasons that, in the last years of his life, Romero became marginal to the institutional Church, although he had the highest ecclesiastical position in El Salvador. He was opposed by all of his brother bishops except one, Rivera y Damas, who was his auxiliary bishop and a liberal prelate who was never able to rise to the heights of self-sacrifice that were to become the lot of his superior.

Priestly Formation (1930–1942)

In 1930 Oscar entered the minor seminary but the loss of family land and the lack of financial resources forced him to suspend his studies for some time to help with the family's finances. He and his youngest brother, Mamerto, who died approximately a year after I interviewed him, were forced to work in the Potosi gold mine transporting heavy buckets of metal and dirt for up to twelve hours a day. They received only fifty cents in local currency, the equivalent of six cents in American money, for their daily labor. Mamerto expressed great bitterness over the misfortunes caused by the rich swindlers, and he even cried when he related the story to me. He told me that the reason Oscar hated the rich was because he suffered so much at a very early age from their greed and exploitation.

Mamerto spoke to Father Rafael Urrutia, Romero's Vatican-appointed "Defender of the Faith," or what formerly was known as "The Devil's Advocate," whose job was to find fault with candidates for canonization. In this case, however, I was later to interview Father Urrutia, who denied this was accurate. I had the impression that Father Urrutia was trying to exalt Romero's memory and exonerate him from normal human feelings. The formal process that eventually led to Romero's canonization began in 1993 when the Archdiocese of San Salvador created an ecclesiastical tribunal to study Romero's homilies, writings, and personal letters, as well as receive testimonies regarding Romero's years as archbishop. Father Urrutia dismissed the possibility that Romero could have been angry with the speculators and said that Mamerto was wrong because Romero was a totally kind and forgiving person. His being kind and forgiving does not necessarily preclude his feelings of anger and righteous indignation, or his having been deeply affected by their familial tragedy. So-called negative feelings, however, may have remained unconscious and only come to light when faced with the repression that took away his best friend, several priests, and innumerable members of his flock. More on this later.

For Oscar, as for many, the Church was the only way in which bright, sensitive, and idealistic young men could find a way to obtain a good education, build a career, and make a significant contribution to society—at the expense of vowing to forego sex altogether for the rest of their lives. Allegedly, the Church and religion could even provide a way to sublimate feelings of lust, anger, and aggression toward social injustice. This kind of teaching would change radically later with the emphasis provided by liberation theology, but at the time Oscar was recruited to attend minor seminary religion was a matter of upholding the status quo and turning the other cheek. Aggressive and sexual feelings had to be suppressed, if not repressed, by the candidates to the Roman Catholic priesthood. The celibate was the ideal image of a man of God, for at the time Protestant churches had not made significant inroads into the traditionally Catholic country.

There is little to suggest that Oscar deviated from the pre-Vatican II ideal of unquestioning obedience to the hierarchical superiors and adherence to traditional theology and piety, which was focused on individual rather than social transformation. This strictness is one of the traits most often mentioned by the people who knew him as a young seminarian and priest. Indeed, it was a trait that earned him the antipathy of most other seminarians and young priests, who allowed themselves certain liberties in the hierarchically imposed ecclesiastical discipline, such as wearing civvies, having drinks, and consorting with female friends.

If we were to use a colloquial term, we might say that Oscar was a "goody two-shoes," which did not endear him to his colleagues but certainly won the admiration of his superiors. Early on in his training he was seen as someone being groomed for high office. His strict discipline seemed to have included some elements that may appear extreme to us, like the use of a sharp wire device called the *cilicio*,[14] which was wrapped around an

arm or a leg and caused constant pain as a means of disciplin-
ing the flesh. He may still have used this device even in his later
years; after his death one of these contraptions was found in
the drawer of his bedside table. Possibly he still adhered to the
practice of kneeling by the bedside in the middle of the night.
He was often seen kneeling in the chapel.

It may seem paradoxical that a man who had suffered
considerably at the hands of the people and institutions that
the Church supported and represented became their faithful
servant. Romero's initial compliance could have been a kind
of "reaction formation"[15] or perhaps a form of "sublimation,"[16]
psychological mechanisms that may prove helpful in defusing
negative feelings. At any rate, a year and a half after he was
transferred to the San Salvador seminary the docile, faithful,
promising seminarian was sent to the Gregorian University
in Rome to train for the priesthood in the most prestigious
Catholic center of learning.

The next chapter will deal with the most productive and
well-documented stage in the life of Romero encompassing
the birth of liberation theology and his so-called conversion. I
believe it is worth considering the use of Erik Erikson's concept
of *moratorium* to understand his remarkable transformation.
Erikson emphasised the role of a psychosocial moratorium
(sometimes called an identity crisis) regarding one's role in
society, values, and commitment. Sometimes it involves cog-
nitive dissonance, which is the incompatibility of one's beliefs
with one's actual feelings and behavior. The moratorium
involves experimentation (for example, adventure, travels,

trying different jobs and professions) and often leads to identity achievement and the commitment to social responsibilities. As we will see, the cocoon of ecclesiastical security gave way to a very different kind of priest and human being, one that has captured the imagination of millions for over four decades.

CHAPTER 3
MINISTRY AND MARTYRDOM

Priestly Ministry (1944–1970)

At the time Romero began his priestly ministry, El Salvador, the smallest country in Central America, was the most over-populated nation in Latin America. It was also one of the poorest. The monthly minimum salary was $168 and the cost of basic food for an average family was $150 a month. With the conversion of local currency to US dollars, inflation soared to the point that a family of four—which would be the exception since families tended to be larger—needed at least $600 a month to live modestly. Combined unemployment and underemployment had reached 72.5 percent.

Conditions in the countryside were appalling; most people suffered from malnutrition and were practically illiterate. Most Salvadorans lacked potable water and access to medical care. Fifty-three of one thousand infants died before reaching one year of age. In an agricultural country where survival depended on land tenure, one percent of the population controlled seventy-one percent of the farmland. Half of the country's income went to 8 percent of the population. One hundred families controlled the economy in a country of six million people.

The origins of El Salvador's sharp inequality can be traced to colonial times, when the Spaniards concentrated the best lands in the hands of a few landowners. Prior to the Spanish conquest the Pipil people inhabited El Salvador. They were related to the Mexica (Aztecs). There was also influence from the Mayans in Guatemala. From the Aztecs, Salvadorans inherited a combative and entrepreneurial spirit and from the Mayans, a religious and inquisitive bent.

The Spanish conquistadores brought with them priests and monks who, unlike the Puritans in North America, sought to convert the native peoples instead of physically exterminating them. The Catholic Church formally declared that the natives were human beings and the king of Spain sanctioned marriage among his subjects and the local indigenous women. This is not so surprising given that Spain has been the most racially mixed country in Europe. The Goths and Visigoths blended with Jews and Arabs and with all the array of peoples wandering the shores of the Mediterranean.

In the process of forced conversion, the native Pipils' temples were destroyed, the people subjected to slavery, and their lands expropriated. There was a minor alleviation in the fact that the Spaniards brought very few women with them; only a few noblemen brought their spouses. The rest took native wives or concubines and produced a population of *mestizos,* or people of mixed descent, which mitigated the severity of Spanish rule since the offspring of the Spaniards were also related to the local people.

Octavio Paz,[1] a distinguished Mexican writer, has hypothesized that the *mestizaje* has been a source of conflict among Latin Americans. Since we descended from both European and native peoples, we are apt to either feel allegiance to both or reject one culture in favor of another. We experience contradictions in being children of the oppressors and the oppressed. During the Salvadoran Civil War, many of the revolutionary cadres were of middle or upper-middle class, and predominantly European descent. The children of the middle class rebelled against the oligarchy by siding, at least tactically, with the people of indigenous descent; others, usually the more well off, chose to disown their native heritage by identifying themselves as white. Such are the conditions of most countries in Central America, with the exception of Costa Rica perhaps because land tenure took a different form with the predominance of small landowners.

Romero was conversant with the misery and degradation of the poor in his country and yet he remained silent until the events of 1977. As I will show at the end of this chapter, this was the only period of Romero's life for which we have more personal information because this was when he began to dictate his diary into a small tape recorder. His homilies were taped and transcribed. The archbishop belonged to a predominantly oral culture and wrote very little except for his pastoral letters, and those were done with the assistance of others—mainly the

Jesuit theologian Jon Sobrino—and a few letters of standard pastoral advice to individuals and couples.

Unlike religious figures like Luther, Teresa of Avila, Therese De Lisieux, and Ignatius of Loyola, Romero did not engage in elaborate introspection. His diary and other writings deal almost exclusively with the events in El Salvador, particularly in his diocese, and have a strong social and political flavor. I have drawn extensively on the interviews with relatives and eyewitnesses and the work of previous biographers to map out his trajectory from a pious conservative priest to the archbishop of the people. I have selected some portions of his writings and incidents that stand out as having a particular psychological or psychohistorical relevance.

According to biographer Jesus Delgado, when Romero returned from Rome in 1943, and after a short period of rest in his native Ciudad Barrios, the bishop of San Miguel assigned him to the parish of Anamoros, a small and relatively unimportant village. His younger brother Gaspar, who accompanied him on this assignment, told me they went to the village on horseback because there was no other form of transportation to such a remote location. There was no electricity or running water. They had to fetch water from the river to bathe and drink. At the time, the water was still not heavily contaminated.

Romero stayed in that post less than a year; because of his potential and obedience, he was transferred to the provincial capital of San Miguel by the end of 1944. There he was appointed simultaneously to three positions: secretary of the diocese, rector of the church of Santo Domingo, and priest in charge of the church of San Francisco. Given the age and personality of the titular bishop, the humble Monsignor Machado, Father Romero practically ran the diocese. His appointment to San Miguel was an important promotion that predicted an auspicious career. The church of San Francisco was the shrine of Nuestra Señora de La Paz (Our Lady of Peace) who is the patroness of El Salvador. Delgado describes how Romero fell in love with the image of the Virgin Mary:

> "Oh those eyes . . ." wrote the young parish priest, ecstatic before the beauty of the image of the Virgin of Peace. In his heart was born, and he cultivated, an out of the ordinary religious sensibility towards the Virgin Mary. Each year, on the occasion of the feast of the Virgin of Peace, father Romero dedicated a composition to her in which he expressed the abundance of his tender devotion and revealed the affection of his heart towards such sweet mother.[2]

It is hard not to make a connection between the Virgin Mary and the ongoing attachment to his long-suffering mother Guadalupe de Jesus, her first name being a popular appellative for Mary in Mexico and Central America. His mother was the earthly woman to whom he was also devoted and who accompanied him until the day she died.

In San Miguel, Valladares described Romero as a man who "was on the go at all hours . . . he would work without stopping until he was totally burned out." Father Valladares, perhaps his only friend at the time, said, "This guy stresses himself out by getting so angry! He blows his top so easily he's going to spend his entire life suffering from one sickness or another . . . he would just burn up on the inside and we'd often see him ill at ease, nervous or depressed."[3] Maria Lopez Vigil says that Romero's colleagues described him as, " 'A stickler, that priest! You have to walk around on eggshells with him!' He was a stickler, a *guisthe*. Like one of those sharp slivers of glass that will cut you. Very, very strict . . . that *guishte* as they called him, bothered them so much that they tried to marginalize him. He would get depressed. I started to become aware of the difficulty of his situation."[4]

He seemed to have had a soft spot for alcoholics, however, particularly the street ones. Vigil says, "The drunks were the ones who sought him out the most. They say his brother Gustavo had drinking problems and died of it, and that he had gone staggering drunk around the streets of San Miguel and that everybody knew it. They say he would come to the parish looking for his brother Father Romero, and that Romero would scold him, but that he also had a lot of patience with him. And with drunks you have to have a lot of patience because they will drive you crazy!"[5]

It is interesting to note how his siblings also gravitated toward the brother they perceived as the strongest and how, in a long-suffering way, Oscar had replaced his mother in bearing the brunt of the family's calamities. Guadalupe Romero managed to support the family after they were dispossessed and worked as a laundress even with a partial paralysis that only allowed her to use her right hand.

Oscar also offered to help Gaspar by paying for him to finish high school, but his younger brother, who in some ways was stronger than he was, refused because he did not want to become an additional burden. Gaspar was proud and self-sufficient. He was the brother who recovered at gunpoint the stolen patrimony that Oscar had counseled to forego because of his religiously inculcated disregard for material things.

In San Miguel the weight of his ecclesiastical and family responsibilities took an early toll on the overly responsible clergyman and son. At times Romero questioned his own sanity. His friend, Father Inocencio Alas, related that during a trip to Mexico, "one night he came into my room, all discouraged and hanging his head. 'Father Chencho, tell me. Do you think I am crazy?' He sat down, and it was apparent that he had come for a heart-to-heart, even though that wasn't his style."[6] Unfortunately, Father Alas's narrative ends there.

Romero was described at the time as a scrupulous and traditional priest who did nothing against the will of his bishop, and who always consulted the Church's official teachings before making any decision. He was sought out by the laity, both rich and poor; the former because he dined with them and allowed them to mitigate their consciences by making charitable donations, and the latter because of his paternalistic attitude and the contributions that he gave them. But he was very unpopular among his brother priests to the point that they petitioned the bishop to depose him of all his positions. The bishop made no public statement, but took it seriously enough to admonish

Romero on the matter, advising him to be more attentive to the needs of his colleagues, especially the younger ones.

Oscar moved his mother to San Miguel to take care of her and have her close by. It seems he depended greatly on her for emotional support. He visited her every day. A neighbor commented:

> You could look at her face and see that mother and son looked exactly alike. Her face was his face. Her hands were his hands. You could see that the way she gestured with her hand; was the same way he moved his. Maybe his jaw was more pronounced than his mother's but even that trait he got from her.[7]

Let us remember that his mother's left side was paralyzed and that she only had the use of her right hand. Perhaps, it was a mimetic gesture of his mother that one can see in pictures and videotapes of Romero preaching that he gestured almost exclusively with his right hand, whereas many orators and preachers, right-handed or left-handed, use both hands to emphasize their points. His mother died while he was a priest in San Miguel. His entire family arrived for the burial. A witness remembers, "We saw what they were like—of humble bearing."[8]

San Miguel was the longest tenure of his entire ministry. He already admired Jesuit spirituality while serving there and practiced the retreats prescribed by them but he stayed away from the progressive social and political positions of the Jesuits. Instead, he was a devotee of Monsignor Josemaria Escrivá de Balaguer, the founder of the controversial religious order of the

Opus Dei.[9] Upon Balaguer's death, Romero wrote a letter to the pope advocating for his beatification and subsequent canonization. Critics have described the Opus as a Catholic mafia that conspires to place its members in key political posts in order to exert its conservative influence. They typically target highly sophisticated middle- and upper-middle-class people. A senior educator told me that the Opus controls the Ministry of Education in El Salvador.[10]

I can testify to the appeal of the Opus Dei. Its founder Monsignor Escriva wrote a series of spiritual pamphlets that served as a guide and inspiration for many young people. They consisted of maxims that were short, clear, and demanding; they were a challenge for Christians, young and otherwise. The Opus owned a big beautiful colonial mansion in a residential neighborhood that students were allowed to use for study and prayer. I used to go there and take advantage of the silence and space.

Romero's piety made the Opus a natural place for him, although toward the end of his life he would withdraw from its influence. Fernando Saenz Lacalle, a priest from the Opus, was Romero's personal confessor and later succeeded him as archbishop. The name Lacalle in Spanish means "the street," so the saying was that since the appointment of Lacalle, a right-wing Opus Dei clergyman, as archbishop, the Salvadoran Catholic Church was "on the street."

Romero's care for the well-being of his soul was not matched by a similar care for his health. According to Delgado, Romero subjected himself to unreasonable schedules that caused him to suffer from bouts of anxiety, tension, and irritability. Oscar's emotional distress manifested itself in, among other things, a tendency to frequently correct and admonish the other priests. As noted above, I interviewed Father Delgado at the austere, hot, and spartan offices of the Catholic archdiocese. During our interview Delgado noted that Romero exerted himself to the point of exhaustion in any endeavor that he undertook. This is a characteristic he displayed often, particularly during the more politically agitated years. At times this emotional state of anxiety and tension was described as nervous exhaustion.[11] Brockman writes more extensively on the matter:

> Romero's retreat notes show that as early as 1966 he was consulting a doctor over the stress that he experienced in his life. He noted in January of that year that he had left the retreat house to seek his confessor and his doctor during the retreat. The latter, he noted, diagnosed him as a compulsive obsessive perfectionist,[12] and the retreat notes show Romero fervently proposing for himself a detailed reform of his daily life, which seems to bear out his perfectionism or—in traditional ascetical terminology—scrupulosity.

In Mexico in November of 1971 he noted down his faults as he saw them: avoiding social relations with others, not getting to know people, concern about being criticized, perfectionism, disorder in his work, lack of austerity, lack of courage in speaking out and defending his opinions. In February of 1972, he began Lent with a retreat in Mexico City and noted down at greater length his view of himself in light of his experience of over a year as a bishop and almost thirty years as a priest, now seen with greater maturity and after three months of psycho-analysis, which he viewed as an instance of God's providence in his life. He saw in himself a certain timidity flowing from subconscious attitudes transferred from his childhood to his adult relationships.[13]

Although he had developed a good, even somewhat saintly, reputation with his superiors and with the faithful in the diocese of San Miguel—he was already considered a very good preacher—Romero continued to experience numerous difficulties with colleagues in that same assignment. He was overbearing with the other priests, and even displayed his authoritarian tendencies with his bishop, Monsignor Machado, whom Oscar implored to restrain his sermon, which was reputedly lethargic, to ten minutes, while Romero himself kept on talking sometimes during the entire Mass. Because of his affection for Oscar the humble prelate complied with Romero's request.

At that time the Roman Catholic Mass was said in Latin. Although in theory the Mass was a communal celebration, the fact that the priest stood at a distance from the people with his back turned to them and spoke in an ancient dead language made it look like something mysterious and private. The people experienced it more as a ritual that the priest performed on behalf of them than as common worship. It was not unusual for a preacher other than the celebrant to speak in a voice-over manner while the ceremony continued to be carried out *sotto voce*. As a seminarian I used to assist my parish priest in explaining to the people over a microphone what the priest was doing while he carried on in Latin.

Oscar's charity and activism were proverbial. Salvador Barraza related to me the story of a boy whom Romero picked up from the street and helped to obtain a high school education. In gratitude the boy used to shine Romero's shoes before he went out. Decades later in San Salvador, a distinguished gentleman climbed down from an expensive car and stopped Romero as he walked down the street. He asked Romero if he recognized him, and Romero said no. Then he said, "Father you need to shine your shoes before you go out." Immediately Romero identified the man, and he was much moved. The boy had become a successful professional. A similar story is related by Brockman:

> Raul Romero (not a relative), lived in Romero's house from 1952 to 1955 in a relationship, common in Latin America, of employee-foster son. Raul was fourteen in 1952 and had known Father Romero through catechism class from the age of ten or twelve. The boy helped with housework and received a home, support, and education. When he was seventeen, Romero helped him enter the seminary in San Salvador, which he later left.
>
> Raul recalled Father Romero as both kind and demanding. In catechism class he would question the children about the previous Sunday's gospel to encourage them to listen during mass. . . . Raul remembered him as cheerful and agreeable but capable of showing his anger if, for example he was not given a phone message.[14]

At the time, few people in El Salvador questioned a priest taking younger boys under his roof and there were few reports of sexual molestation or abuse in those circumstances. It was obviously a good arrangement to help the boy and to have him as a home companion and aide.

It was during his tenure as a priest in San Miguel that Romero met Salvador Barraza, a traveling pasta and shoe salesman. Barraza was a dedicated layperson who converted because he witnessed one of his relatives being miraculously healed. He felt attracted to Romero because of his sermons and gradually developed a friendship with him; they used to have meals together and Romero invited him to his rectory to rest and relax. Later, because of his self-employed status, Barraza served as a non-stipendiary chauffer for Romero, because he thought Romero was a lousy driver. In spite of some difficulties arising from Romero's temper, the friendship with Barraza survived until the last day of his life.

Winds of Change (1962–1968)

The most significant event in the twentieth century for the Roman Catholic Church was the Second Vatican Council called by Pope John XXIII, which started in 1962 and ended in 1965. The council called for the updating of the Church (Italian: *aggiornamento*) as an attempt to relate it to the modern world. The Council drew strong criticism from conservative priests. Some, like the sedevacantists, claimed that the Church had fallen into the hands of Freemasons and communists and that Pope John

XXIII, who called the Council, was an impostor. The conservatives saw the introduction of Marxist analysis and humanistic enlightenment notions into religious thinking as a modernist conspiracy. Romero read the documents issuing from the council, analyzed them carefully, and was made uncomfortable by innovations arising from them. It was the opening provided by the council that made allowances for the priests' relaxation of ecclesiastical discipline, and prompted them to ask the bishop to remove Romero from San Miguel. Brockman writes:

> Though Romero evidently saw the council as a personal call to himself as a priest of the church, he by no means sympathized with all the tendencies that appeared in the church after the council. Young priests who appeared without cassocks, even without any sign of their priesthood, who were familiar with women, who were so restless to change the church and the world—all met with his disapproval. By now he was long established as the most powerful priest in the city, with virtually all lay movements centered in his parish, besides being the bishop's secretary, rector of the minor seminary, and editor of the diocesan newspaper. Other priests resented his monopoly of power coupled with uncompromising attitudes and severe ways.[15]

One may surmise that at this point Romero had become a kind of "power freak." He seemed obsessed with control and had succeeded in running the most important institutions of the diocese. He also broadcasted his sermons on five radio stations in the small provincial capital. When the bishop went away, Romero was in charge. However, in spite of his popularity with the laity and hierarchy, the tensions between Romero and the other priests reached such intensity that he was relieved from his posts. In 1967, a few months after the twenty-fifth anniversary of his ordination to the priesthood, the bishop gave him the title of Monsignor and transferred him to San Salvador to be the secretary of the archdiocese, which Romero, given his hierarchical bent, probably appreciated.

Journalist Maria Lopez Vigil relates the testimony of a humble woman who was present at the farewell ceremony.

We thought he would be the new bishop of San Miguel . . . But he was not appointed as bishop nor allowed to stay in San Miguel. We never knew why, but the order arrived that he had to go to San Salvador to work as secretary to all the rest of the bishops.

The farewell party took place in a movie theatre in San Miguel. A lot of people showed up, standing room only. Poor, rich, half-rich and half-poor arrived at the event. Everybody. I dressed up with the best I had, my light blue dress, but as soon as I came in I felt embarrassed. There were a lot of big ladies there, all wearing fancy clothes.

What I remember the most from that event was a boy who climbed up to the stage where he was, with a sheep to give it to him as a gift. Father Romero received the sheep. When we saw him carrying the sheep we all clapped a lot. Even I clapped and my godmother clapped also. So did the big ladies who had congregated there to praise him.

And in the middle of the celebration I looked intently at Father Romero. . . .

Do you want me to be honest? Father Romero? Friend of the poor and friend of the rich. To the rich he said: love the poor. And to us the poor he said: love God, He knows what he does putting you at last; you will have the heaven later. And to that heaven he preached to us would go the rich who gave alms and the poor who did not rise up. . . .

Father Romero? He went with the sheep and he also went with the wolves and his thinking was that the wolves and the sheep we should all eat together from the same plate because that is what God likes.

Those were ugly times. The coffee barons, the big cotton farmers, the cabal of the Garcia Prietos, they ate all the lands of El Salvador and they drank our sweat in exchange for a few pennies, the ungrateful ones. And so many people still unconscious like asleep, thinking that no one can change this thing, that it was the will of God.

I looked then at Father Romero up there on the stage carrying that baby sheep. But, honestly I think if he would have been presented with a little wolf with fangs and all, he would have received it the same.

Everyone clapped and there was a lot of corny crying because he was leaving. After twenty-three years he was leaving San Miguel. As far as I am concerned, I cannot say that I was really sorry about it.[16]

Delgado says that in being transferred to San Salvador Romero was "promoted, but removed."[17] It was a manner of honorably and discreetly disposing of a hard working but problematic cleric. As noted above, at his arrival in San Salvador Romero, while still being a priest, was given the title of "Monsignor" which applies both to bishops and distinguished clerics. The title became almost synonymous with his name. In 1967 Romero arrived at the Seminary of San Jose de La Montaña, which was run by the Jesuits, where he chose to set up his office. There he was to meet Father Rutilio Grande who became his best and, perhaps, his only close friend at the time with the exception of Barraza. Rutilio was also known for his introverted personality and his scrupulosity, and it has been said that Romero and he were a good match for each other.[18]

San Salvador: Beginnings of Romero's Episcopate (1967–1974)

According to Brockman, upon his arrival to the capital city of San Salvador Romero was seen in his office at the seminary until very late at night. Lopez Vigil describes Romero at the time as:

> A LITTLE INQUISITOR trying to investigate and persecute, to condemn to death, any new movement that was trying to take root in the Seminary (where he lived), in the community of the Jesuit Fathers who ran the seminary; among the priests themselves, and in the church in general; he saw it as his prerogative as secretary general of the bishop's conference.[19]

The superior of the Jesuits has still harsher words for him:

> I didn't like him. He was an insignificant human being, a shadow that went by clinging to the walls . . . People were talking about his psychological problems back then. They said he took trips to Mexico to recover . . . He had his world and it was not like ours. He started off on the wrong foot from the very beginning. . . .
>
> Miguel Ventura, a seminarian, also called him "a perfectionist." They say he never took his eyes off the floor. The Jesuits who taught at the seminary and ran it also lived there. One of them told me that one day he found Romero practically cowering against the wall, with the wind knocked out of him. When he saw him so upset like that he said, "Monseñor, what's the matter with you?" Romero was so frightened that he could not even talk.[20]

His allegiance to the traditional institution, however, really paid off. Between 1917 and 1980 the population of El Salvador quadrupled to five million. In the introductory chapter I mentioned the archbishop of San Salvador, Luis Chavez y Gonzalez. He was a pious and gentle but courageous cleric whom I met and saw on numerous occasions. Chavez had known Romero for quite some time and asked him to be his auxiliary bishop. Chavez y Gonzalez was also known as an example of the monarchic episcopate, inasmuch as he was traditionally pious, hierarchically oriented, and fond of pomp and ceremony. However, he was to precede Romero in accepting liberation theology. According to some, Chavez laid the groundwork and provided the basis that would make it possible for Romero to follow in his footsteps. The old archbishop is a good example of how the radical seeds of the gospel message can give rise to unexpected results.

Chavez was known for being cozy with the government and even allegedly supported a repressive episode. Asked by President Jose Maria Lemus if he should use force against a popular revolt, Chavez is purported to have answered in the affirmative, because he, as the president of the Republic, had been empowered by God to do so.[21] He followed the interpretation of the "two swords" mentioned in Luke 22:38 as meaning that the two powers came from God, that is the church and the state. Chavez was an old-fashioned cleric formed in an intense ascetical tradition. He must have worn the *cilicio* and flagellated himself, and like Romero he was often seen at prayer. However, unlike his successor, he was interested in developments in church doctrine and consistently fostered innovation in the archdiocese. Sister Luz Cuevas, the superior of the Carmelite order who hosted Romero at the hospital for cancer patients during the time he served as archbishop, told me how a rich lady asked her to intercede with Cardinal Casariego to recommend Romero as the new archbishop. The reason she alleged was that they could not tolerate the liberalism of Archbishop Chavez any longer.

After much soul searching and an intensive retreat Romero accepted the appointment as auxiliary bishop but doubts about his own intentions and purity continued to plague him. Brockman says that in a retreat he made in Mexico around that time Romero questioned whether he had been mature enough when he accepted the call to priestly celibacy.

At that point, Romero was consulting a psychiatrist regularly and the latter diagnosed him as suffering from an obsessive compulsive disorder (OCD); later, he also saw two Jesuit psychiatrists who confirmed the OCD diagnosis. They counseled him with finding secure environments and making a daily schedule in accordance with his realistic possibilities. Romero's perfectionism was so extreme that he accused himself of *sacrilege* for not saying Mass with the appropriate devotion. The latter concern was technically irrelevant since the Catholic Church believes that the efficacy of the Mass is valid *ex operae operato,* that is, regardless of the purity or holiness of the priest presiding. Evidently, one of his main concerns was the undertaking of celibacy and his ability to keep it perfectly. His self-doubts were most likely due to the persistency of his natural sexual inclinations.

Psychology asserts that obsessive-compulsive behavior is a way of dealing with intense but unexpressed feelings. Freud even went as far as seeing an analogy between religion and obsessive-compulsive neurosis.[22] He also pointed to the need to perform certain rites as a means to achieve a feeling of inward purity. So, we must ask what kind of feelings tormented Romero and drove him to that type of behavior. Unexpressed anger and libido can have this effect. In Oscar's case his strict religious formation would have prevented him from openly expressing or even acknowledging those feelings.

As expected Romero elaborated a detailed schedule that would seem excessive to most clerics and may have even exacerbated his OCD. Romero wrote in his diary that he would abide by the following purposes:

I.   To strengthen my interior life:
  a)   Sincere return to piety:
    1.   Daily meditation (I will follow the thought of the liturgy or fall back on the eternal truths in time of temptation).
    2.   Examination of conscience. (After siesta, and a brief one before lunch.) I'll make the particular examination on my problem of protection and the general on this reform.
    3.   Breviary and spiritual reading. Continue as they are.
    4.   Go back to saying the rosary in church. Invite those in the house to the Rosary Association.
    5.   Go back to making the monthly spiritual retreat.
    6.   Thanksgiving after Mass.
    7.   Weekly confession. I'll go see Father Damián, set the day, and prepare it better. Saturday when going or coming back from hearing the confessions of the hospital Sisters, or whatever day Father chooses.

After thus outlining his "return to piety," he goes on:

b) Give a characteristic of penance and mortification to my duties.

1. Organize better the time for attending to all my duties: parish, diocesan office, printing shop, seminary, other works and associations.

2. Order in my accounts. Get them up to date and pay off my debts this year. Especially to the Soler family. [It is not clear if this refers to personal debts or to the finances of his parish or other works.]

3. Charity and humility. Not speak ill of anyone, and no self-praise. Not let in the idea of vanity. Love and pray for those who do me or who I think do me wrong. At least observe common charity. Hold out some hope of reconciliation and union.

4. Overcome my harsh and grim disposition. Attend with kindness those who come to see me. Especially with priests, seminarians, the poor, the sick. Even a refusal can be given with kindness.

5. Custody of the eyes: newspapers, the confessional, the street.

6. On Fridays and Saturdays some small fasting or mortification at table in honor of Christ's passion and of the Blessed Virgin. Abstain from sweets.

7. Wear a penitential chain (*cilicio*) from rising after siesta until after prayer.

8. Discipline on Friday nights.

So far, he has outlined his plan to strengthen his interior life. He continues his proposal of reform:

II. Environment of protection.
1. Not travel alone to San Salvador—or stay in a dubious lodging.
2. Let someone else take care of answering the door.
3. Confide my problem to my confessor [presumably, the "problem of protection" mentioned in 1.a),2].
4. Keep certain persons at a distance.
5. Await the circumstances of the future, hoping for the best solution. [I think this refers to the effect a change of bishop in the diocese will have on Romero's future, a matter he had written about elsewhere in the notes.]
6. Avoid solitude.
7. Have an outing with companions (*compañeros*) (I think he means other priests, seminarians) once a week.

Romero's 1966 schedule was modeled after the type of asceticism that prevailed in Catholic religious orders and seminaries before the Second Vatican Council. The Catholic priesthood is essentially monastic. The problem consists in the fact the diocesan clergy lack the community support and schedule provided by monasteries and Catholic seminaries; that is why Romero found it very difficult and frustrating to maintain his strict discipline, especially as it concerned celibacy. He noted his "harsh and grim" disposition, but such a disposition is not surprising considering the pressure he was putting on himself to conform to the type of asceticism he outlines in this retreat diary. Note that he was aware both of the disposition that he showed to people and of his doctor's diagnosis of his personality. Yet he does not seem conscious of their relation to the type of asceticism he was bent on practicing. Brockman observes:

> I think that the psychiatrist may have suggested to Romero that his obsessive-compulsive perfectionism was shown in an excessive concern about chastity . . . that a way out of his obsessive perfectionism was to let some external cause take hold of him ("another object can be given to my obsessive-compulsive perfectionist personality"). . . .
>
> But his focus was still too much on himself and on the details of his ascetical practices. In November of 1968, he made another retreat and again mapped out a plan of life like that of January of 1966, although somewhat shorter and less detailed. It was only as archbishop, years later, that he would become caught up in the cause of the poor and the defense of justice. Then, his excessive focus on himself would diminish.[23]

On June 21, 1970 he was ordained to the episcopate. The president of the Republic, many civil officials, and numerous people from his former diocese of San Miguel attended the event. Clergy and lay leaders in the archdiocese were displeased with the selection due to the dominant tendency of the day to apply the liberal directives of Medellin and of the Second Vatican Council to the reality of El Salvador. Six years later this opposition was to become even fiercer in the wake of his elevation to archbishop. Romero was perceived as the worst choice for the people and the best choice for the ruling elites.

Shortly after his elevation as auxiliary bishop, perhaps due to the stress and inner conflicts surrounding the event, Romero fell ill with fever and coughing. Barraza took him to his home in San Salvador. Barraza was then married to a woman named Eugenia. The two nursed Romero back to health. Many distinguished visitors came to pay their respects. Father Peyton, the aforementioned director of the Rosary prayer crusade,[24] and his Opus Dei confessor visited him there. While convalescing, Romero celebrated the Eucharist at the dining room table, with Barraza's eight-year-old adopted daughter, Lupe, serving as an acolyte. I spoke to Lupe about her relationship with Romero and she told me that when she was eight years old she used to scold and pester (Spanish: *regañar*) Romero for his lack of compliance and disregard for his good health. The Barraza home became the place where he relaxed, kicked off his shoes, stretched out on a reclining chair, watching TV on Sundays after Mass as he sipped a drink of whisky. Later he became the *compadre*, that is the godfather, of Lupe, a relationship that is strong and binding in Latin countries. Romero and Barraza would travel to Mexico and Guatemala. He would talk to the Barrazas about his sorrows, and once he even cried at the dinner table while he related the attitude of his brother bishops against him. Barraza proudly told me once that people used to think they were brothers. However, Barraza knew that his friend could be short-tempered and difficult. Once he stayed away from the Barraza family for several weeks because Barraza was late for an appointment to drive him somewhere. In a country where punctuality is not precisely a virtue, Romero became tired of waiting and took a cab. When Barraza arrived, he was already gone.

After Romero's death, Barraza left Eugenia, who was older than him and in ill health, and he partnered with Martita, the daughter of the family's domestic employee, who was a young and beautiful indigenous woman. Later, Barraza petitioned Rome to have his first marriage annulled on the grounds that his first wife had been unable to bear children.

The annulment finally arrived and twenty years later, in 2001, he married Martita. During all this time he was forbidden to receive Holy Communion and he complied with the rule. Leaving an ailing elderly wife for the maid's daughter does not seem to be exactly the kind of behavior one would expect from the archbishop's closest friend. His daughter Lupe spoke to me with great bitterness about her father's actions and has apparently been unable to forgive him completely. Perhaps his friendship with Romero helped him keep the family intact; after his death, however, he felt free, as he explained, to follow the dictates of his own heart.

In 1972, because of the Jesuits' controversial theological teaching (that is, their support for liberation theology), the hierarchy, with Romero's prompting, decided to relieve the Jesuits from running the seminary and for the first time in Salvadoran history diocesan clergy were placed in charge of it. Romero was named rector of the newly reconstituted institution. Too much money was spent at the outset with a very small enrollment; the institution became very difficult to maintain, and only six months later the new seminary was closed. The collapse of the seminary was a dispiriting event for Romero because it constituted a major failure of management.

As had been true in San Miguel, Romero was overextended. He was still auxiliary bishop, editor of the diocesan newspaper, and secretary general of the bishop's conference. Because the school was more expensive than other comparable ones, Bishop Aparicio pulled his students out; this made the institution impossible to maintain. The big gray building located on a hill on the outskirts of San Salvador became a kind of ghost town with so few students. Although other factors had been involved in the closing, such as the ineptitude of the vice rector Father Freddy Delgado and the lack of cooperation from Bishop Aparicio, Romero, as the captain of the sinking ship, took full responsibility for the failure. Romero was transferred and named bishop of a newly formed diocese in El Salvador, based in the remote town of Santiago de Maria.

These were very difficult years for the country. An electoral fraud in 1972 set off a widespread wave of massive protests. The government decreed martial law and unleashed an intense campaign of armed repression and political persecution. The new president, Colonel Molina, a personal acquaintance of Romero, inaugurated his term with the invasion and takeover of the National Autonomous University. People were brutally beaten with rifle butts and about eight hundred students were imprisoned. On the church side of things Romero launched a campaign to attack the Jesuits. Expelling them from the seminary he tried to have them removed from the Externado de San Jose, a middle-class high school run by the Jesuits. The Jesuits were furious and considered him an outright enemy. The provincial of the Jesuits describes an exchange that took place at that time:

> "Look," I told him rather angrily, "you are accusing us of very serious things and I want you to tell me what you are basing these accusations on" . . . I discovered that even though he waged heated battles he was really a timid man . . . He kept his eyes downcast and responded simply: "I have reliable sources of information. . . ." He didn't look up.[25]

It is interesting to note that instead of being penalized for the failure of the seminary Romero was rewarded by the hierarchy he so dutifully served, by being appointed a diocesan bishop and relieved of his auxiliary post. This reinforces the impression that he enjoyed the personal predilection of his superiors even when his performance was poor and not well received by others. Up to this point, Oscar displayed the kind of obedient and submissive character and deference to persons in authority that will lead to promotion and protection, even in the face of his unfavorable performance and results.

In 1974, the bishops chose Romero as their delegate for a synod in Rome. Romero refused the election and resigned and the bishops then designated Monsignor Rivera, his auxiliary and loyal supporter, who was the alternate. Then Romero changed his mind and said he wanted to go. The matter was referred to the Vatican who confirmed Rivera as the delegate, causing a certain stress between the two prelates. It seems as if his wish to be humble and refuse the honor clashed with his desire for recognition and the latter finally, though untimely, prevailed.

Oscar was here showing that he was capable of a drastic turnabout, a foreshadowing of his change in the last decisive years of his ministry. He did not succumb to the pressures of the—increasingly dominant—liberation theology elements. It was rather as if he matured a personal conviction and eventually acted on it.

At this point we have to take into account the fact that Romero had been faithful and consistent with the basic evangelical tenets, as he understood them, in terms of his inclination to help the poor. In San Miguel he took under his protection boys from the street and gave them an education. He also allowed poor coffee farm workers and the poor to spend the night at the rectory. His understanding of the gospel mandate was to provide charity, assistance, and relief without upsetting the status quo. Most people I interviewed talked about Romero's reinterpretation and reenacting of his Christian faith as the work of the Holy Spirit. But the doctrine of the incarnation that the Catholic Church ascribes to teaches that the Holy Spirit does not operate in a vacuum. Grace builds on nature and personal and historical events predispose people to the action of the Spirit. Otherwise history becomes irrelevant to the plan of salvation. Apparently, this was the case with Oscar.

Initial Conflicts (1974–1977)

In 1974 Romero was appointed bishop of the diocese of Santiago de Maria. This was a big coffee growing location in the eastern part of El Salvador. It was a new diocese that included his native town of Ciudad Barrios; Romero was its second bishop, and he found himself in a peculiar situation. A substantial percentage of priests operating there were older than he. Possibly out of respect for their seniority, he was not as directive and critical of them as he was with his younger subordinates. Instead, the relatively young bishop was a kind of maverick who took to the streets and remote villages in a vehicle equipped with powerful loudspeakers to preach and administer the sacraments. Although Romero had been accused of being too comfortable with the big coffee landowners, he was already expressing some concern for the well-being of the coffee harvesters, the worst paid seasonal workers in the country. In an issue of *El Apostol (The Apostle)*, a weekly publication from the diocese, he wrote,

> It saddens and concerns us to see the selfishness with which means and dispositions are found to nullify the just wage of the harvesters. How we would wish that the joy of this rain of rubies and of all the harvests of the earth would not be darkened by the tragic sentence of the Bible: "Behold, the day wage of the laborers that cut your fields, defrauded by

you, is crying out, and the cries of the reapers have reached
the ears of the Lord of hosts."[26]

Brockman adds:

Romero's concern for justice for the harvesters is evident
amid the flowery language, but he offers no solution for
the injustice beyond wishing that the landowners were not
so selfish and fraudulent. After he became Archbishop, he
would come to recognize that the oppressed must organize
in order to pressure for their rights, and he would vigorously defend the rights of their organizations.[27]

The quote can be seen as either some kind of evolution in
Romero's thought or simply a statement of traditional church
doctrine and Holy Scripture that has always called the unjust
rich to repentance with highly questionable success. Very few
of his rich parishioners went beyond throwing a Christmas
party for the workers and giving their children cheap toys. The
coffee barons and other rich people gave no wage increases nor
improved working conditions.

There was an incident during his tenure in Santiago de Maria
that tested his ability to respond to the new theological trends.
In that location, liberation theology priests were carrying out an
evangelizing experiment called *El Naranjo* (The Orange Tree).
Peasants were taken to a retreat center and taught the liberation-
ist doctrine of Medellin. The teaching had an intense antiestab-
lishment, even anti-government, flavor. To the conservatives the
teaching's intensity resembled brainwashing. In addition, one of
its leaders was Father David Rodriguez, a popular priest who did

not belong to his diocese and had participated in an occupation of the cathedral. Romero was very troubled by this particular experience. A Spanish priest who served as a missionary at that location remembers being told by Romero:

> "The teaching you do is too participatory." That's what Monseñor would say most often when we could talk about the work at Los Naranjos center. He had finally let us open it again. Sometimes he would come at me with another kind of argument. "I've heard that the government is worried about this type of teaching too." . . . The man would get so nervous; he'd develop a tick. The corner of his lip would start trembling. It would shake and shake, and he couldn't control it. Really, hearing about Medellin, and having his lip tremble was one and the same thing. In this particular juncture Romero gave evidence of a talent for compromise in a way that, more or less, pleased or at least appeased everyone. He diluted the focus of the center, but he did not annul the experiment. He decentralized the theological reflection groups by ruling that parish priests must supervise them. *El Naranjo* experiment earned him the admiration of the hierarchy and the government, both of which saw it as a proof of the new bishop's talent for compromise. In addition, although he was not yet under the sway of liberation theology, he created the impression of being somewhat open to the Medellin directives, thus ingratiating himself with the more progressive elements. At that time the government had not caught up yet with the full implications of the liberation theology teaching.[28]

A more disturbing episode, however, clouded his last years as bishop of Santiago de Maria where he served for three years: the *Tres Calles* (Three Streets) incident. According to Brockman, in that location a group of peasants returned from a meeting with their Bibles under their arms. They were intercepted by a group of National Guard who opened fire with their machine guns and killed them instantly. The guards alleged that the peasants were carrying subversive weapons. According to other witnesses the peasants were dragged out of their homes and shot in the middle of the night.[29] Those of us who lived in El Salvador at the time can testify about the terror inspired by the cruelty and arbitrariness of the National Guard, which can be compared to Mohammad bin Salman's in Saudi Arabia or Somoza's reign of terror in Nicaragua. The killing of these peasants gave rise to widespread popular outcry. Romero was asked by the grassroots lay workers and priests to intervene and denounce the massacre; instead, he chose to inquire privately with President Molina and be discreet about raising the issue of official government intervention. His handling of this incident endeared him to the coffee barons of the area and the business and high-society people in the capital city of San Salvador.

It was from during that time he served at Santiago de Maria that Father Macho relates a most peculiar incident. A conservative priest came to Father Macho with a message from Romero that the classes of a certain radical priest at El Naranjo center should be suspended immediately. Father Macho went to see Romero and confronted him at once; it was then that the unthinkable happened. According to Macho, Romero fell down on his knees and begged him for forgiveness, "He felt so confused . . . that he got down on his knees in front of me. And when I saw him humbling himself that way, I picked him up from the ground and hugged him."[30] It is unclear why Romero felt the need to ask for forgiveness. Perhaps it was a way of appeasing Father Macho, who was described to me by Salvador Barraza as a very high-powered individual—as he put it "a big burly Spanish priest."

The incident is another instance of Romero's kneeling behavior that looks like a manifestation of masochistic self-abasement and self-immolation. It is also interesting to note that the last name of the priest involved in this incident is *Macho*, which means "virile," "manly"; whereas, with his perpetual wearing of a cassock, thick glasses, and demure demeanor, Oscar was not the prototype of a macho man. Romero may have felt he was compelled by the Christian imperative to seek forgiveness; the kneeling, however, was obviously a rather excessive way to act it out.

In 1975 the Vatican appointed Romero as a consultant for Latin America. It was a major distinction for a newly appointed bishop. He attended a meeting in Rome and reported about the political activities of the Jesuits and how they were infecting the seminarians and students with their political theology. However, he exonerated his friend Rutilio Grande who, according to him, did not agree with the actions of his confreres.

Because of progressively leaning to the side of liberation theology teachings, Monsignor Chavez became undesirable to the influential right wing. The old man had to go. Chavez was a priest formed in the same mold as Romero. Notoriously pious, he was said never to smile or appear without his cassock. Bishop Barahona, a seminarian under Chavez, concocted a plot with another seminarian to see him without his cassock. The seminarians knocked on the door of Chavez's bedroom after the bishop had retired with the pretense of asking for a good night blessing. The bishop opened and lo and behold he was wearing pajamas. In this manner they were able to achieve their mischievous purpose.[31] After consulting with the people in power, the papal nuncio decided to recommend Oscar Romero to succeed Monsignor Chavez as head of the Archdiocese of San Salvador.

The newly appointed archbishop returned to San Salvador in March 1977. He immediately felt the rejection of the priests and nuns, who greeted him politely but coldly. In an effort to elicit their support he made a few concessions about liberation theology doctrine, more in terms of being charitable and advocating for the poor than of denouncing the injustices committed against them. Again, it was not just a matter of the deprivation the people suffered in the countryside and working-class sectors, but of the widespread violation of civil and human rights and the arbitrariness of the so-called security forces, supported by the US government, that systematically prevented any kind of trade unionism or organizing.

Metamorphosis (1977)

On March 12, 1977, something happened that would change the course of Salvadoran history and Romero's life in a decisive way. Jesuit priest Father Rutilio Grande was driving to the town of El Paisnal, in the vicinity of Aguilares near the capital city of San Salvador, when he was machine-gunned along with two peasants who accompanied him. Romero showed up immediately with a group of priests at the location and celebrated a Mass. Those who saw him at the time relate that they had never seen him so grieved and upset. He seemed at a loss for words and was unable to speak. A witness remembers:

> It was midnight when Monseñor Romero arrived to see his body. He approached the little table where we had him, wrapped in a white sheet, and there he paused, looking at him in a way that made me see that he loved him too. I didn't know Monseñor then. That night we heard his voice for the first time preaching. When we heard him it was a great surprise. "Ay! Even his voice is just like Father Grande's." That's what we said.[32]

It became commonplace to call Romero's change *El Milagro de Rutilio* (Rutilio's Miracle). Many people considered that in one way or another Rutilio's death had been the catalyst for his transformation; some even understood the "miracle" in a mystical sense—as God's passing on Rutilio's spirit to Monseñor.

Father Grande was to be the first in a long list of murdered priests brought down by government repression to quell liberation theology. That very same day President Molina called Romero to express his sympathies for the loss. It had already been determined that the weapons used in the murder were of the kind used exclusively by the armed forces. Later, Romero commented bitterly on the cynicism of the president.

The day before the murder Romero had encouraged Father Grande not to withdraw from his pastoral work in that location, in spite of the threats and the enclosing circle of doom. At a clergy meeting held on March 10, 1977, he told Rutilio, "Since you are all Jesuits, I don't think anything will happen to you. Go on back to your pastoral work on Sunday, and don't worry. And sometimes we should talk about this experience of Aguilares during these last few years."

Rutilio responded, "I hope we can Monseñor, God willing."[33] It was the last time the two friends would see each other alive. We may surmise that this unfortunate advice was a particular cause of guilt for the archbishop.

Practically speaking it was the turning point. One hypothesis is that the death of Rutilio triggered in Romero what became popularly known as his conversion.

The priests of the archdiocese rallied around the archbishop and counseled a most daring course of action to protest the killing: to cancel the celebration of the Eucharist at the level of the entire archdiocese, and to hold a single Mass in the Cathedral of San Salvador. Romero's decision to follow through with this unprecedented recommendation was a landmark and truly astounding one. He was a man who agonized even about smaller decisions. In this case Romero would have to go against the nuncio and his brother bishops. Father Ibanez remembers his struggle:

He was smaller than ever. When the last meeting about whether or not to hold the single Mass was over, his brow was more furrowed, he was more withdrawn, more anxiety-ridden than ever. He had said yes to the idea, he had accepted it, but who knew how much criticism he would have to face. After leaving Guadalupe Hall, four or five of us priests stayed around talking to each other. We lit our cigarettes and started exchanging our impressions. "The man has changed."[34]

He also consulted with Father Alas, who responded to him with what, in my opinion, was pure Anglican ecclesiology because in Episcopal polity the local bishop is the ultimate arbiter:

> You and only you are the bishop. And you are the one who must answer to God for the decisions you make as pastor of this people. God has given you this charge, and He has given you the responsibility for the Archdiocese of San Salvador. The nuncio does not have this responsibility. Not even the pope has this responsibility. It is yours alone.[35]

The next Sunday a massive single Eucharist was celebrated in San Salvador with the attendance of more than a hundred thousand people. The same Father Alas describes what happened then:

> The priests dispersed into the crowd, and hundreds of people were saying their confessions on the streets. Many

people who had distanced themselves from the Church for years, returned to their faith that day. Rutilio's assassination and the message given by that single Mass were alarms sounding, waking people up. As the Mass began, I noticed that Romero was sweating, pale and nervous. And when he began the homily, it seemed slow to me without his usual eloquence, as if he was reluctant to go through the door of history that God was opening for him. But after about five minutes I felt the Holy Spirit descend upon him. . . . "I want to give public thanks today, here in front of the archdiocese, for the unified support that is being expressed for the only Gospel and for these our beloved priests. Many of them are in danger, and like Father Grande, they are risking even the maximum sacrifice. . . ." Hearing the name of Rutilio thousands exploded into applause. . . . Thousands of people were applauding him, and something rose within him. It was then that he crossed the threshold. He went through the door.[36]

The lines were drawn. From that moment onward the archbishop was no longer seen as the ally of the military and the ruling classes but as their biggest opponent. The single Mass took place on the twentieth day of March, scarcely eight days after the tragedy. Unless we want to attribute such drastic and rapid change exclusively to the death of Rutilio, we have to consider whether in fact Oscar had not already pondered the questions involved in the church's response to governmental violence and how his character and background sustained this change.

The People's Prophet (1977–1980)

At his arrival in the capital city Romero had felt isolated and rejected. With the exception of Barraza, Rutilio was his only friend. But his friendship with Rutilio was more egalitarian. The two men were one of a kind; they both were described as having reclusive and nervous personalities, and they sought each other for comfort and support. It appears that the depth of their mutual affection was, if not the decisive factor, a very crucial one in motivating the latter's change, and it can be no accident that it happens to appear at the crossroads of Romero's transformation. Like Oscar, Rutilio was born in a small rural village to a family of small landowners and knew poverty as a child; also, like Romero, he suffered from pathological scrupulosity. An anonymous writer describes him as follows:

> The first signs of [Rutilio's] nervous weakness were evident in Quito and in the two subsequent years in Panama and San Salvador. During those years he was affected with a serious mental weakness. In 1965 his superior informed that he was still suffering from tensions and certain anxieties, which at their worst prevented him from working effectively. He had a major proclivity towards perfectionism. This, sometimes reached insane levels. Five years later, in 1970, his superior reported psychological depressions caused by the state of his nerves.[37] Apparently, this constant weakness produced in him an instability of criteria and decisions. Some people who knew him during the last years of his life narrate that it was difficult to speak with him when he was going

through one of these psychological depressions. This was compounded by the diabetes which he developed in the last years of his life. Sometimes both ailments conspired to produce in him very difficult emotional states.[38]

The same author also narrates that Rutilio went through a particularly bizarre period of scruples shortly before his ordination to holy orders, to the point that he almost postponed the ceremony altogether. He only went through with it after his spiritual director ordered him to do so. Nevertheless, he had to write a statement saying that he wanted to go through with it even if doing so meant that he was committing a sin. It is practically impossible to understand the obtuse logic of this behavior unless we see it as a serious case of obsessive-compulsive personality disorder. This is the psychological profile of the first martyr of El Salvador and Romero's predecessor and best friend. They were like identical twins. Like Romero, Rutilio was also traditionalist and rigorous when it came to church doctrine and morals. Also, like Romero, he transformed himself and went into a kind of trance when he was at the pulpit. They were both known as great preachers. Apparently, this ancient sign of power and authority acted as a shield and a prop for them and somehow made up for what the two men were lacking in their everyday social intercourse.

Perhaps to mitigate his loneliness after Rutilio's death, Romero petitioned the sisters who ran the Divine Providence Hospital for terminal cancer patients to live with them. A sister showed me the tiny closet-like room behind the sacristy where he used to sleep until they built him a small house on the grounds. The building of Romero's house was carried out in secret lest he would prevent the nuns from doing it. Day by day the archbishop would see construction work in progress but never suspected it was for him. One day suddenly they surprised him and gave him the keys. Romero reluctantly agreed provided that he would occupy only one of the three tiny rooms and the rest would be used for guests.[39] Again, he was following the model of the classic Catholic saint and subjecting himself to the practice of the asceticism of poverty. It was an example of what has come to be known as "white martyrdom"; if the early church ideal was to imitate Christ in his martyrdom and the express way to sanctity was to lay down one's life, the second best was white martyrdom, that is to renounce the world and all its pomp and glory. It is possible that, in some way we do not understand, this type of asceticism and self-abasement prepared Romero for the ultimate sacrifice. A video recently released by the canonization office of the archdiocese says that in addition to the *cilicio*, Romero also subjected himself to flagellation as a form of discipline.[40]

Upon his return to San Salvador a priest relates another instance of kneeling behavior when he was trying to repair the Catholic radio station. The priest technician was about to leave for an overseas trip when the bishop summoned him because of his expertise. He reluctantly agreed to stop by.

> I went solely out of a sense of obligation. I didn't know Romero from Adam. Cesar introduced me, and told him I had experience, that I knew a lot about radio. . . . Monseñor Romero looked at me and said exactly these words: "I am

asking you to help me save the radio station. And if I have to, I'll get on my knees." No one had ever gotten on their knees to ask me for anything. Much less a bishop! But the tone of his voice made me feel like he might just kneel down right there in front of me! It really threw me for a loop. It moved me. "Bring on that radio, Monseñor," I told him. I didn't even remember to cancel my plane reservations.[41]

The last three years of Romero's ministry were characterized by relentless confrontation with the established authorities and the gradual physical elimination of his priests; sixteen in total were killed during the conflict. In his homily of April 30, 1978, he questioned the integrity of certain judges whom he accused in a sermon of taking bribes. This sermon is a good example of the kind of detailed denunciation the archbishop carried out consistently.

We can't forget, that there is a group of lawyers seeking amnesty for political prisoners. They have recently published the reasons that moved them to struggle on behalf of so many people who are perishing in the jails. These lawyers are also denouncing anomalies in the procedures used in the criminal courts where the judge is not allowing the defendants to have their lawyers present. Meanwhile the National Guard is allowed to enter and to drive fear into the hearts of the prisoners, many of whom show clear signs of torture and these guards allow the prisoner's state of mind to continue to be influenced by his tortures, that is not acting justly. I think brothers and sisters that these injustices can be seen all around us—in the criminal courts and in many of the other courts of our people. Not to mention in all the judges who accept bribes! What is the Supreme Court doing about all of this? Where is the transcendental democratic role of this branch of government? It should be above all the other branches, calling them to demand that those who are violating the law be brought to justice. I believe that this is key to understanding a large part of the troubles of the nation.[42]

The government took him at his word and requested him to provide them with the names of those judges so they could investigate them. Romero consulted his own lawyers who advised him to obviate the request because it constituted a trap so that he could be accused of slander. Romero refused to provide the authorities with any details alleging that he was not the one called to do it. Instead of ignoring the challenge as his lawyers had advised him to do Romero denounced them again:

I am not the one who should be naming the people the Supreme Court could investigate. They could use for example the information provided by the well-known groups of mothers and family members of political prisoners, of the disappeared and the exiled. They could also use all the denunciations of corruption published in the media, not only in this country but all over the world . . . without any doubt, even more troubling than the cases of corruption, there are these other cases that illustrate the Honorable Supreme Court's absolute disregard for the obligations ascribed to it by our constitution, obligations that all of its members are required to fulfill.[43]

His lawyers were astounded: "He didn't pay any attention to us! He came out swinging—just the opposite of what we told him to do!"[44]

Because of the ongoing censorship, Romero continued to be the only source of news and information regarding human rights abuses. His Sunday sermons enjoyed the broadest radio audience, surpassing even the broadcasting of soccer games, this particular sport being a national craze in El Salvador. Another priest commented on the way his words became increasingly more relevant:

> At first, Monseñor's presence was more important than his words. But little by little, his words took on more and more importance. . . . It was like he was afraid of what he, himself, had said. And when he was afraid this habit of his would start: he'd hook his index finger in the collar of his cassock, and move it back and forth, this way and that way. He was a coward and he knew it. He was a prophet, and he didn't know it.[45]

This body language, like the tick described above, was likely caused by the anxiety and stress of a man who was fond of solitude and was thrust into a public position of vast responsibility.

It is important to keep in mind that he was facing severe attacks on the church in particular. The death of Father Rutilio Grande was followed by the assassinations of Frs. Ernesto

Barrera (November 28, 1978), Octavio Ortiz (January 20, 1979), Rafael Palacios (June 20, 1979), and Alirio Napoleon Macias (August 4, 1979). He did not live long enough to bury Father Manuel Reyes, who was killed after him on October 7, 1980, and the six Jesuit martyrs of the Catholic University (November 16, 1989). In this regard I also have to raise the question of whether Romero did not experience survivor's guilt and to what point this may also have been a force leading to the desire for martyrdom as a kind of expiation.

Brockman[46] describes an incident on Monday April 3, 1978, that exemplifies the kind of defiance that in the climate of the times led to his becoming the prime target for the right-wing opposition. This time he defied the rest of the hierarchy, the people who could have presumably provided cover and support for him.

The crisis was triggered by a group of priests who met weekly with Romero's consent, and occasionally with his presence. They sent a letter to the papal nuncio Archbishop Emanuele Gerada that had been signed by approximately two hundred priests and religious out of the 1,125 functioning at the time in El Salvador.

Although the nuncio had presided at the funeral Mass for Father Grande, the letter did not acknowledge it. Instead, the letter accused the nuncio of acting in a manner unworthy of a Christian by taking sides with the rich and powerful while failing to advocate for the poor and oppressed. More specifically, they condemned the nuncio's celebrating the Eucharist with a priest that had been removed by Romero, while abstaining

from attending the funeral of Father Navarro, a priest who had
been murdered for his defense of human rights.

It was a strong letter; the undersigned priests and religious
prayed that the nuncio would not "keep struggling against the
light and truth in the service of Caiaphas, Herod, and Pilate."[47]

I was struck by the fact that Romero came unabashedly
to the defense of the priests in question, and confronted the
Salvadoran Conference of Bishops on their behalf. Here is
what he wrote in his diary for April 3, 1978:

> The Bishop's Conference of El Salvador called an urgent
> meeting. . . . it had to do with the matter of the letter
> from the priests to the nuncio and I could therefore, by
> attending, give an opinion in defense of the priests. . . . the
> document written by the priests should itself be analyzed,
> not just to criticize the composition or the inadequacy of
> expression, but rather to see concretely what the nuncio
> has done to cause them to say that his witness is less than
> Christian.[48]

From a standpoint of diplomacy or dialogue, it could be
argued that the priests' letter was indefensible. It was unreasonable to think that the nuncio would respond in a positive
manner. He would have had to be a saint, but that is precisely
what the authors of the virulent letter were accusing him of *not*
being. The same objections could have been presented in a different manner without inflammatory language. The archbishop
himself could have presented those same objections personally
to the pope's representative with more tact and sensitivity. The

letter was provocative and seemed designed to close the doors to any kind of meaningful dialogue.

The outcome was predictable; Romero was outnumbered four to one. The bishops voted to reprimand the priests who had signed the letter in question and to publish a rebuttal. To compound matters the other bishops attacked the archbishop and accused him of inciting violence and playing into the hands of the communists. In Romero's own words:

> Bishop Aparicio took advantage of the occasion to say that what I defended in the priests against the nuncio was the same thing I was doing with the dioceses of El Salvador; that my preaching was violent, subversive; that it was dividing the clergy and the dioceses; that the priests now looked more to the archdiocese than to their own bishops.
>
> I do not remember how many more accusations he made that were also supported by my brothers: Bishop Barrera who also called my preaching violent; Bishop Alvarez who took the opportunity to voice his disagreement with me; and the strangest part was that Bishop Revelo, recently named my auxiliary bishop, also took the opportunity to disagree with my approach.[49]

Even his own auxiliary bishop Monsignor Revelo voted against him. The latter, whom Romero chose to be his auxiliary, was a man who harbored mixed, if not outright hostile, feelings against him. Monsignor Revelo had attacked him publicly, and yet Romero went ahead with the appointment. One cannot help but think of the relationship between Jesus and Judas. Was the archbishop unwittingly setting up the stage for his own martyrdom?

We know that the incident hurt the archbishop very deeply. Brockman says that, according to Romero, "The day left a sour taste," and adds that, "The meeting must have been a rough session for Romero. The Barraza family recalled that Romero had at least once wept when mentioning his problems with the other bishops after one of the conference meetings, and this may have been the occasion."[50]

This was the spring of 1978, two years before Romero's martyrdom. We know that the circle was already closing in on him and that he had to face the recalcitrant nature of the army and government. It had been almost exactly one year since his friend, Jesuit Father Rutilio Grande, was assassinated on March 12, 1977. Was this some kind of "anniversary reaction"? It is also interesting to note that Romero himself was murdered almost exactly two years later (March 24, 1980). This was also the time when, because of the variable date of Easter, Holy Week was also commemorated.

At this point it was most likely clear to the archbishop that, unless he chose a route other than direct challenge and confrontation, he would be the next on the hit list. His famous pronouncement that if he were to be killed he would rise in the Salvadoran people bears witness to this certainty. The results were disastrous and counterproductive. The little rapport that was left between the two prelates was essentially lost.

Romero acted in this and similar circumstances with boldness and assurance and an unusual moral certainty and lucidity. The archbishop found himself in a situation akin to that described by philosopher Jean-Paul Sartre in his play *Dirty Hands*.[51] It is Sartre's contention that the French were never as free as during the German occupation of their country, the reason being that at that time the choices were clear, or at least clearer than usual. You had to decide whether to side with the invaders or to militate with the resistance. The situation in El Salvador during the years of the civil war was similar. A very small and extremely wealthy elite, with the backing of the U.S., used a corrupt and bloody army to crush the aspirations of the extremely poor majority for freedom, dignity, and human rights.

Romero's course of action makes sense from the standpoint of his Christian faith and values, but we may also wonder whether he was not also driven by a death wish. This would be consistent with the masochistic way in which he responded to challenge and provocation, such as in the kneeling behavior that we have quoted above. He also appears to be identifying with his suffering mother who had been despoiled by a rich swindler. I do not believe it is necessary to postulate an opposition between psychological and religious motivations. I do not question that the archbishop was motivated by a profound love for his people and that he sought to imitate Christ in his sacrifice. The Christian response is characterized by being willing to lay down one's life instead of taking someone else's.

However, we cannot say with certainty that he was not depressed, in fact we have plenty of evidence that this was indeed the case. Self-immolation may have, at some level, appeared to him as a desirable alternative, given the amount of psychic aggression and conflict that had to be internally negotiated. Romero must have been furious and in deep mourning. Given Romero's conscience and principles, physical retaliation and aggression were out of the question. Since he was a celibate, he was forbidden to be sexually intimate with another person who may have comforted and supported him. His loneliness may have constituted an additional source of frustration and depression.

The question is whether a sacrificial faith stance motivated by love can be or need be totally exempt from *Thanatos*, the drive that inexorably impends us toward death. After all, according to the drive theory, the death drive is the other side of *Eros*, that is, the lust for life and the desire for existence; the two drives are deeply intertwined. Perhaps there is an element of the death drive in willing martyrdom, or at least in being able to accept death for the sake of a greater good. This does not detract from the value of sacrifice, but may well be in the very nature of it. Perhaps this is a way in which the archbishop expressed the rage and grief caused by the death of his beloved friend, Father Grande, and of so many of his priests and laypersons. It may also have been a way in which he actualized the love and concern he felt so deeply for those entrusted to his care.

In one of his last collected statements the archbishop referred to the spiritual kind of purification needed to imitate Christ, but the extended meaning cannot be disregarded; he is talking about his own death and immolation. On March

19, 1978, six days after the confrontation with the bishops, he wrote:

> Holy Week is a call to follow Christ's austerities,
> the only legitimate violence,
> the violence that he does to himself
> and that he invites us to do to ourselves:
> "Let those who would follow me deny themselves,"[52]
> be violent to themselves,
> repress in themselves the outbursts of pride,
> kill in their heart the outbursts of greed,
> of avarice, of conceit, of arrogance.
> Let them kill it in their heart.
> This is what must be killed.
> this is the violence that must be done,
> so that out of it a new person may arise,
> the only one who can build
> a new civilization:
> a civilization of love.[53]

His stances in regards to his brother bishops and to the papal nuncio seem paradoxical if we consider that, faithful to his name ("Romero" means one who goes in pilgrimage to Rome), he consulted the pope's teachings assiduously and went to Rome often in search of advice and support. His relationship with Pope Paul VI was very good. In their last meeting Pope Paul VI had told him to have *coraggio* (courage); he said, *you are in charge.*

His meetings with Pope Jean Paul II were not so successful. When he went to Rome after having made an appointment to see him, he was denied an audience. He had to take advantage of the pope's weekly appearance at the solemn Sunday Mass to hurl himself on him and to force him to listen. However, in spite of the pictures of murdered priests that he showed him, the pope admonished him severely and told him the best he could do was to work for a more harmonious relationship between the church and the Salvadoran government. At one point he even questioned whether the murdered priest was not perhaps a guerrilla. All of this came from a man who as a cardinal in Poland had been one of the main opponents of the government. Paradoxically, Jean Paul II decried injustice and advocated for the poor. Perhaps it was the pope's anticommunist fears that occasioned such severe reaction.

The wealthier classes in El Salvador portrayed Romero as the main instigator of the war. Apparently at times he was so abrasive that we may have to wonder if his style did not do something to earn him that reputation. We have to ask why he went about it with such vengeance. Could he have supported the demands of the poor and denounced injustice without going to the extremes of calling for the soldiers to disobey orders or making statements that seemed to threaten the rich? Romero went so far as to describe the use of violence against the rich, even in such graphic ways as saying that they should take their rings off of their fingers and give them to the poor or else their hands would be cut off. After speaking about the popular social project, he goes on to talk about the opposite plan, that of the rich:

> Finally, the other political project is that of the oligarchy, they are trying to organize and expand their forces to protect their interests. Again, in the name of our people and of our church, I am issuing a new call for them to hear the voice of God and gladly share with everyone their power and riches, instead of provoking a civil war that will drown all of us in blood. It is still time to take off your rings so that your hands will not be cut off.[54]

Such a lurid image as the mutilation of rich people's fingers could be interpreted as a threat of castration. A ring is also a symbol of riches, of belonging, of power, and of loyalty, in this case to the upper class. Romero himself wore the conspicuous episcopal ring and as far as I know he never took it off. The menacing tone also points to Romero acting as the harbinger of the civil war that was indeed to soak the entire nation. Was the archbishop expressing the sense of powerlessness that the people felt by being deprived of the most elemental rights? Was he channeling their frustration at being deprived of any legitimate channels to bring about change? And, was he also expressing a personal grief and rage, something that had been brewing inside him and could only finally come to fruition in crisis?

A few weeks later, he explained:

> Nothing is so important to the church as human life, as the human person, above all, the person of the poor and the oppressed, who, besides being human beings, are

also divine beings, since Jesus said that whatever is done
to them, he takes as done to him. That bloodshed, those
deaths, are beyond all politics. They touch the very heart of
God. As a pastor, I invite you to listen to the hoarse, imper-
fect echo of my words. But do not regard the instrument;
regard the one who bids me tell you of God's infinite love.
Be converted! Be reconciled! Love one another! Fashion a
people of the baptized, a family of God's children! Those
who think that my preaching is political, that it incites to
violence, as though I were the cause of all the evils in the
land, forget that the church's word does not invent the evils
in the world; it casts a light on them. The light shows what
is there; it does not create it. The great evil is already there,
and God's word wants to undo those evils. It points them
out, as it must, for people to return to right ways.[55]

His sensitivity to injustice was made evident in an incident narrated by the sisters at the cancer hospital, in which he
confronted a group of North Americans that had arrived with
a donation. Romero was having lunch when they approached
him to make conversation. This is what happened next as
related by one of the sisters:

> . . . Monseñor was not allowing himself to be engaged. He
> hardly talked at all. He just kept eating and listening to the
> news. When the news came about a robbery, one of them
> decided to try that topic.
>
> "There is so much crime. Really! There are a lot of
> thieves in this country!"

"People have every right in the world to steal if they don't have anything to eat." Monseñor cut her off suddenly and looked at the three of them in the eye. "The first right of a human being is the right to eat. If they can't eat, then let them steal."

It was so sudden, so abrupt and so direct that the three Americans' eyes opened wide with shock. No one argued with him. They just turned so pale that they ended up whiter than they already were. An absolute silence followed, and without even finishing their food they got up from the table, said a cold good bye to Monseñor and left. I went with them. They hadn't even gotten as far as the garden when they exploded.

"That man is full of hate and violence! They warned us that he was a troublemaker."

When they got back to their "society" they voided the check they'd already written. Ten thousand dollars!

Monseñor Romero knew very well that they'd come to give a contribution and that it would be a big one. I don't think the gringos understood what happened.[56]

I can think of many ways in which he could have raised the North Americans' conscience without antagonizing them so abruptly, for example simply quoting a few statistics that showed why some people are so desperate that they see no other way but to resort to thievery.

His detractors pointed to the fact that the civil war started shortly after his assassination and that he spoke openly of the right, even the duty, to take up arms in the face of tyranny. Most upper-class Salvadorans I spoke to referred to him as "a murderer," meaning I assumed, that his sermons incited others to resort to violence. One successful and otherwise proper professional even told me unabashedly that, given the opportunity, he would have been the one to shoot him. Their perception of the archbishop by the upper and middle classes would be more similar to Osama Bin Laden than to Jesus, Martin Luther King, or Mahatma Gandhi.

In fact, Romero's message was not unequivocally pacifist but a reinterpretation of the Catholic doctrine of "just war"; in this case one that included the right of rebel groups to take arms. Traditional doctrine had applied the just war doctrine to the right of duly constituted governments to declare war in justifiable cases, such as the war against Nazi Germany. His interpretation of just war allowed guerrilla groups to assert that Romero justified their actions and to claim him as a poster figure. The left and the poor canonized him, while he was still alive, as the greatest defender of their rights.

The truth of the matter lies somewhere in between the extremes of defensive aggression and impeccable sainthood. As per the *simul peccator et iustus* (a sinner and saint at the same time), principle mentioned above, Romero embodied the ideals generated by the Second Vatican Council and significantly reinforced by the Medellin Conference in Colombia that gave rise to liberation theology. There is no question in my mind that he loved the people entrusted to his care and was deeply concerned about their rights and their well-being.

He was personally shaken, however, by the murder of so many of his priests, especially Father Rutilio Grande, and by the repression unleashed against his church. He must have, naturally, harbored feelings of anger in the face of the damage inflicted, feelings of grief in view of severe personal losses, and feelings of guilt because of his impotence to change the situation. All of these combined may have contributed to his decision to forego caution, lash out against the perpetrators, and perhaps also to contemplate martyrdom as the most desirable option.

Doubts about himself and about his behavior continued to plague him until the end. One day Father Urrutia, who was later to be in charge of the initial investigation for his canonization process, found him in tears: "Help me," he told Urrutia. "If you can show me that I am wrong, I will get down on my knees and ask the Salvadoran people for forgiveness."[57] One more time we see that in the gesture of submission represented by kneeling, Romero found comfort and relief from tormenting feelings. A year before his death he arranged for another psychiatric evaluation, this time incognito, in which he pretended he was a married businessman with many responsibilities. In the end the psychiatrist caught on to the game. Romero's fictional presentation of himself should give pause to question the results of the evaluation:

> He decided to make a trip to Mexico, but its purpose was disguised. He was going to get a checkup. "Do me a favor," he said to some friends. "Find me a good psychiatrist who

can do an evaluation. But I don't want the doctor to know who I am. This is the only way he'll feel free to say what he thinks, and I'll feel better about it that way." Monseñor Romero was hanging by a thread. He was afraid he was losing his mind, he was apprehensive about losing control over the archdiocese and he felt like different groups of people were trying to manipulate him at different times. . . . "My fear is that I won't be able to meet everyone's needs, and I am afraid of being subject to undue influence by other people. I'm so exhausted, Doctor, that I don't know any more if I'm the one making decisions or if I am being dragged along by other people's desires. . . . I need to know if I'm acting freely, based on my own judgment!"[58]

Although to some extent the arch-episcopal ministry allowed him to set aside some of his former conflicts, it is clear that here he was at the breaking point again and practically overcome with feelings of depersonalization by being pulled in many directions.

While in Rome, toward the end of his life, Romero confided to the superior of the Jesuits why he believed he had changed, and how he thought that his transformation was a return to his roots and also how the change had to do with his friend Rutilio's death:

We were walking down the *Via della Conciliazione*, in the background the dome of the Vatican. It was late at night. I felt that the slight chill, the darkness, were favorable for confidences. I dared to make him speak.

"Monseñor you have changed, you can tell in every-thing you do. . . . What happened? Why did you change, Monseñor?"

"You will see, Father Jerez, I ask myself the same thing in prayer. . . ." He stopped walking and kept silent.

"Do you have any answer, Monseñor?"

"Some, yes. . . . the fact is one has roots. . . . I was born in a poor family. I suffered hunger; I know what it is to work as a child. . . . When I went to seminary and got into my studies and they sent me to finish them here in Rome, I built another world. Afterwards I went back to El Salvador and they gave me the responsibility of being the secretary of the bishop of San Miguel. Twenty-three years I was a par-ish priest there, also very buried in papers. And when they brought me to San Salvador as auxiliary bishop, I fell into the hands of the Opus Dei! That was it."

We were walking slowly; it seemed as if Romero wanted to keep talking.

"Afterwards they sent me to Santiago de Maria, and there I ran into misery again. With those children who died just because of the water they drank, with all those peasants, half-dead from the hardships of their cutting cof-fee labor. . . . You know, father, a charcoal that has been a burning coal does not need much wind to catch on fire again. And then you cannot underestimate what happened when I became archbishop, I mean about Father Grande. You know how much I treasured him, when I looked at him dead, I thought: if they killed him for what he did, I

am bound to go the same way. . . . I changed yes, but also I
returned to my origins."

We continued to walk in silence, the new moon faintly
illuminating the Roman sky.[59]

According to this testimony, two factors emerge very
clearly from Romero's own lips as contributing greatly to his
turnabout: First, his early experiences of poverty and hardship
and his re-encounter with similar situations in his new pastoral appointments. His more consistently liberal colleague,
Monsignor Rivera y Damas, the favorite of the left, was unable
to rise up to the heights of denunciation and militancy that
Romero did, most likely because he was a patrician clergyman
who came from a well-to-do background. Second, his great
affection for Father Grande and the effect his murder had on
him as the newly appointed archbishop of San Salvador. He
even goes as far as to say that he felt he had to go the same way,
to lay down his own life. Was this some kind of logical conclusion or a kind of death wish prompted by survivor's guilt?[60]
Perhaps both.

Consummatum Est (March 24, 1980)

Romero's last days evolved as a veritable passion play. The
attacks of the right wing had intensified to the point that several friends and associates advised him not to go out without
protection. But he refused to accept their advice. On March 23,
1980, he delivered his most famous homily, in which he pronounced the words that have been engraved in history as one

of the most significant discourses in the history of Christianity. At the end of the homily he addressed the people serving in the armed forces, beginning with a call to obey their class origins. Since the draft has not been enforced in El Salvador most men who serve are rounded up by the recruiters among the poor peasants and workers and conscripted by force. He began by giving an extensive account of the atrocities committed in the past week.

One case stands out: the peasant Agustin Sanchez, who had been captured on March 15 by the army in Zacatecoluca and turned over to the customs police, was found on March 20, still alive. Sanchez declared, in a notarized testimony before witnesses, that he was tortured for four days, without food or water, being flogged continually and submitted to asphyxiation. On March 19, along with two other peasants, he was shot in the head. The bullets, however, only destroyed his right eye and cheek. Still alive, he was found in the early hours and received help from other peasants. He could not sign his testimony because both of his hands were destroyed.

On Sunday March 23, Romero preached what would become his most famous homily and the one that would seal his fate:

> I would like to make a call in particular to the government soldiers, and specially to the rank and file of the National Guard, Police, and headquarters. Brothers, you belong to our people, you kill your same brother peasants. In the face of an order to kill given by a man, the law of God that says THOU SHALL NOT KILL must prevail. . . . You have no

obligation to obey an immoral law. . . . We want the government to take seriously the fact that reforms stained with blood are of no use at all . . . In the name of God then, and in the name of this suffering people whose laments cry out to heaven even more loudly every day, I beg you, I implore you, I order you in the name of God: Stop the repression!"[61]

Romero's outstanding oratorical gifts are most evident in this last Sunday sermon. But it was as if Romero had signed his own death sentence. At this point he had given up all premeditated political maneuvers. Romero was even going against the official teaching of the Church dating back to the New Testament (Paul's Letter to the Romans) and elaborated by St. Augustine of Hippo that legitimizes the authority of the state and bestows on it the power to maintain law and order. Only military officers can issue that kind of order. His sermon was the equivalent of calling for a *coup d'etat* and open insurrection. It is at this point that we must consider the possibility that Romero was in fact driven by a death wish in the form of martyrdom. In this context, I believe that we may not necessarily consider a death instinct a negative phenomenon. What are we to make of Jesus Christ and of the way he voluntarily embraced the passion to fulfill what he understood to be his father's will? Dietrich Bonhoeffer, the Lutheran pastor who died at the hands of the Nazi regime, is credited as saying, "When Christ calls a man, He calls him to die."

Romero was keenly aware of the imminence of martyrdom. There is a time when life as we know it ceases to be the highest value and this certainly was the case with Romero. At this point he felt he had to speak up, even if it meant a certain death. This has been the case with the heroes of so many struggles for freedom and independence, but in the case of Romero there is a clarity of purpose and determination that is truly chilling. Romero can be seen as an example of the stuff that Christian martyrs are made of. Suffice to think of the way the first Christians, when given the choice between apostasy and death, preferred to be thrown to the lions in the Roman Colosseum. There is nothing we can say in regards to the faith aspect because normal human categories are insufficient to describe what goes into this kind of choice and the grace and power given to individuals who are capable of making it.

However, it seems as if Romero at that point had reached a conviction that his influence would bring about change in an extremely turbulent and complex situation. Most martyrs do not expect their death to have an immediate political effect. The meaning of Christian martyrdom is highly mystical or spiritual, and its effect will be the building-up of the kingdom of God here and in the hereafter. Their reward is solely a matter of faith.

In spite, however, of the undeniable influence of the Church in a predominantly Roman Catholic country, there was no way in which the Church alone, even its highest representative, could bring about the kind of change that was required. In El Salvador in the late 1970s the odds were overwhelmingly in favor of the US-supported government. Even the already quite strong popular organizations could not challenge the power of the state. After a ten-year war and the occupation of San

Salvador, the capital city with almost two million inhabitants, by the rebel guerrilla forces, the people still refused to rise up in arms, and the army remained loyal to the government.

Some may argue that the course of events was substantially unaltered by Romero's sacrifice, at least in terms of his goals; ending repression and building a more just society. In fact, he is often blamed with igniting a prolonged and bloody civil war. The fact is that a war is not made in a day. Social and political conflict had been escalating for many years, and the popular movements, particularly the armed branches, were built up slowly with the help of the former Soviet Union and Cuba. It was a geo-political conflict. The war ended with a series of negotiations, which did bring about some measure of democratization. The UN reported, however, that an unknown number of people disappeared and seventy-five thousand people, mostly civilians, were killed. At present, abuses at the hands of the security forces continue, only this time aimed at the gangs, or *maras*; military governments gave way to civilian presidents. The leftist opposition who led the guerrilla forces became an opposition party that was unable to win an election until 2009 and was soundly defeated after its failure to bring economic change and social justice; the first leftist president has been accused of corruption and became a fugitive. In a postscript I will go into more detail about the present situation.

Romero pronounced his decisive homily on the day before his death. It was the Fifth Sunday of Lent, a week before Holy Week. We do not know for sure if he was killed solely in retaliation for this particular homily. The calculated crime is likely to have taken more than a day to plan, but this was the sermon that best exemplified his boldness and defiance of the official authorities. On that fateful day, March 24, 1980, he went with some other priests, including the current archbishop of San Salvador, Monsignor Saenz Lacalle, to the beach for a moment of rest and reflection. Romero used to retreat to the ocean, which is less than thirty minutes from San Salvador, for occasional relaxation with his friend Barraza. On this last day he drove with his colleagues and asked Barraza to stay in the city. There was a humorous moment when they arrived at the beach and the resort was locked because the caretaker was absent. Saenz Lacalle went around looking for a place to break in, while Romero was able to climb a wall and jump inside only to find that the caretaker had finally showed up and the place was already open.

After leaving the beach Romero made a stop in Santa Tecla to make a confession with a Jesuit priest at the church of El Carmen. In midafternoon he returned to San Salvador, where he was being awaited to celebrate the Eucharist and preach at the chapel of the Divine Providence Hospital, the same place where he lived. Barraza insisted on accompanying him that day, but he staunchly refused and instead commissioned him to take care of what Barraza describes as "a silly assignment," in making sure a platform for Holy Week services was the right height for the people to watch properly. Perhaps it was a way of keeping his friend out of harm's way. Barraza also told me that the day before his friend's death had been characterized by a pervasive feeling of farewell. Romero spent Sunday afternoon with a youth group and "he seemed to enjoy their company immensely, it was as if he was saying goodbye."

In that last Eucharist he delivered a much briefer homily to commemorate the first anniversary of the death of Mrs. Sarita de Pinto, mother of the owner of the newspaper *El Independiente*. The event had been announced in all the newspapers, and everybody knew that he would be there. He spoke about the relationship between our efforts to improve society and the reign of God:

> God's reign is already present on our earth in mystery. When the Lord comes, it will be brought to perfection.[62]

> That is the hope that inspires Christians. We know that every effort to better society, especially when injustice and sin are so ingrained, is an effort that God blesses, that God wants, that God demands of us.[63]

After the homily, as he offered the bread and wine, a sharpshooter fired a deadly explosive bullet into his heart. It is very moving to see the bloody vestments he wore then. The bullet's entrance is very small but the damage was massive because of the caliber of the weapon used. In seeing these vestments, which are preserved in his former residence, I sensed the enormity of the crime that was then committed.

Romero was rushed to the hospital immediately, but he could not be saved. When Barraza came in, Oscar was already dead. Barraza says he was let in because the hospital personnel thought he was his brother. It has been said that on the way to the hospital Romero stayed conscious barely enough to forgive his assassins; however this, though it is quite likely, has not been confirmed. An autopsy was performed immediately and Barraza witnessed, with great consternation and grief, how he was disemboweled and torn apart. Barraza took his bowels to the yard of the small house where he lived at the cancer hospital and buried them there. The nuns who run the hospital claim that many years later when they exhumed the remains, they were still intact and had not suffered corruption.

In the postscript I will detail the attempts that have been made to investigate the crime. Although it was commonly acknowledged that Roberto D'Aubuisson, the right-wing leader of the paramilitary death squads, was the intellectual author, there was never a single attempt to indict him. He came out on TV and showed pictures of the priests whom he accused of being pseudo-priests, wolves in sheep clothes and communist agents. He was the known founder of the infamous death squads. D'Aubuisson, who was a chain smoker, died a few years later from throat and mouth cancer. Allegedly he was deformed by the severity of the cancer and people stayed away from him because of the stench he emanated. This kind of death was regarded as a punishment for his great sin of magnicide. D'Aubuisson's sister, Marissa, is a devout follower of Romero and attends the weekly Mass held in his honor in the basement of the metropolitan cathedral.

In the conclusion of this work I will explore the dynamics of Romero's transformation from the standpoint of his personal background, his longstanding gospel values, and the radical turn of events that he was involved with during the last half of the turbulent decade of the 1970s. In addition, I will attempt to understand how a man with the psychological characteristics of Romero became—in the face of overwhelming odds—the foremost advocate of the oppressed. On the surface nothing had prepared him for this role. He had been steeped in conservative Catholicism and had had bestowed on him the privileges of the highest ecclesiastical office. By nature, Romero was shy, introverted, even antisocial, and had consistently displayed a tendency to acquiesce to the status quo. Even when his family lands were usurped, he refused to put up a fight and counseled resignation.

I was unable to learn a great deal more about his friendship with Rutilio Grande. The grief caused to him by this close personal tragedy does seem to be a major factor in a change of such magnitude. His humble origins also accounted for his newfound sensitivity to the plight of the poor. From a faith standpoint, we may affirm that supernatural grace was also a factor in Romero's turnabout; however, it is at this point where our inquiry must end. This kind of study can only try to understand his personality; the action of Grace is bound to remain mysterious.

CHAPTER 4
A LIFE'S CONCLUSION

In *Martyrdom and the Politics of Religion: Progressive Catholicism in El Salvador's Civil War* Anna Peterson writes, "After Jesus, Oscar Romero represents the *iglesia popular's* (the popular church's) consensus choice as model martyr."[1] Before the Vatican formalized and monopolized the process of canonization, people were canonized by a generalized popular consensus (*vox populi vox Dei*).[2] This is done to this day in the Orthodox Church. Before the hierarchy initiated the canonization process, Romero had already been declared a saint by popular acclamation. Before his transformation Romero appeared to most people to be the least likely candidate for such distinction. The image of Romero that emerges from this case study is that of a man afflicted with more than a fair share of human flaws and vulnerabilities. Those who knew him closely described him as being far from a model of psychological health. He was lacking in the art of public relations and social skills expected from a man of his position;

it must have been particularly hard for him to function as a figure of international relevance and be constantly in the limelight.

Videotapes of him being interviewed show a short, stocky, and slightly stooped man dressed in a black cassock with a purple cincture who avoided direct eye contact and gave brief responses, sometimes only paraphrasing or parroting the interviewer's questions, such as:

Question: "Are you an advocate for the poor?"

Answer: "Yes, I am an advocate for the poor."

He looked uncomfortable in the glare of the public eye, as if he were trying to get away from the situation. His shyness was legendary, as well as was his lack of close intimate friends.

In spite of all objections, Oscar Romero may be viewed as an example of a person in whom moderate to major psychological problems and holiness *coexisted*. It is often the case that sensitive persons attuned to injustice and suffering are likely to experience a greater difficulty in remaining impassive witnessing the ills of modern society. Their susceptibility may translate into psychological symptoms such as depression and anxiety—both of which were common in Romero, even when he took an active role in fighting against injustice.

He experienced personal hardship early in his life. Witnesses differ in their evaluation of the effect this deprivation had on him. Most assert that, with the true nobility of a saint, Romero forgave and forgot, but his brother Mamerto assured me that Romero "hated" the rich for subjecting them and their parents to such destitution and suffering.[3] Romero himself admitted to Jesuit provincial Father Jerez that the poverty and despair among the rest of his family, particularly his mother, who they allege became ill as a result of the upset caused by the dispossession, left an indelible mark on him.

There may have been some feelings of guilt involved also since his kin lacked the material security that was, and still is, taken for granted by Roman Catholic clergy, who are pampered and supported for life by their bishops or religious order. It is interesting to note that at a time and region where few people had automobiles, the clergy were usually provided with one; this single fact was a big symbol of privilege. Given the reluctance on the part of friends, relatives, and witnesses to talk about Romero's early life, some of the data about particular events are incomplete. This is understandable, as many consider him an anointed one who manifested divine predilection since early childhood. This is a matter of faith, and it is not the purpose of this study to delve into such matters. If the chosen ones are subjected to trials then he did possess that mark, aggravated by persisting psychological ailments. However, we may draw some further conclusions from the available data.

Romero's father was not a religious man; however, he inculcated in young Oscar strict norms of behavior by making sure his transgressing had dire consequences in terms of punishment. Physical punishment was not unusual in those days. There was a great deal of sadism, however, in the way his father punished him severely for minor offenses. Romero became hard on himself later in life, as if he had internalized a tyrannical super-ego.[4] It is interesting to note that his father's name,

"Santos," is the plural in Spanish for "saint," and his mother's name was Guadalupe de Jesus; her first name, as mentioned earlier, was the most popular advocation for the virgin Mary in Mesoamerica, but she was called Jesusita, a feminine diminutive of Jesus. Unwittingly perhaps Oscar actualized in his life the meaning of his parents' names. It was the doctrine instilled by the Jesuits, who were central to his formation, to become a saint by imitating Jesus. Catholic religion in El Salvador has been traditionally regarded as the province of women, older people, or priests. Nevertheless, even dissolute younger men or philandering husbands seem to get some of the fear of God in them toward the end of their lives. El Salvador, in spite of evangelical inroads, is essentially a country imbued by Catholic culture. Overall, we can fairly speak not only of a feminization of Catholicism—most churchgoers are women—but, paradoxically since all the priests are men, of a feminization of the priesthood. Catholic vestments and rituals have a decidedly feminine or at least an androgynous look. Moreover, the stylized liturgical actions and movements do not require qualities that are traditionally associated with masculinity, such as physical strength and prowess, or boldness and courage. They do require, however, qualities that are considered feminine, such as attention to detail and aesthetic sensitivity. Formal celibacy provides a convenient escape, or cover, for men who are afraid or unsure about their sexuality, whether they are gay or straight. We know that Oscar struggled with his sexuality and that as late as on the eve of his ordination to the episcopate he had doubts about having undertaken the vow of chastity.

Because of his father's alcoholic absenteeism, from early on the child Oscar gravitated toward his mother and her interests. Paradoxically, when he played priest and organized mock religious processions, he excluded women. He even wore his mother's apron and pretended that it was a priestly vestment. Romero's attachment to his mother was very strong. His desire for martyrdom to the point of vehemently rejecting protection could have expressed a desire to identify with his suffering mother and morally triumph over the despots.

When the time came for him to choose a profession he went against his father's wishes. Instead of continuing to apprentice as a carpenter, a manly profession that would, in a way, have brought him closer to imitating Jesus of Nazareth, he fought back to be allowed to enter minor seminary and begin preparing for the priesthood. One may wonder if an elementary school boy of that age was already in possession of enough discernment for that kind of option. Later in life, presumably because of his loneliness, he questioned whether he was mature enough when he took the option to be celibate.

Psychiatrist and LGBTQ advocate Richard Isay has convincingly argued the hereditary nature of same-sex orientation. He has pointed out that boys who have a constitutional inclination to homosexuality overwhelmingly tend to turn away from a rejecting father, the impossible and primary object of their love, and effect an identification with the mother. They feel different; they tend to become reclusive and shy away from traditional male games and activities. Their self-esteem is impaired by the father's explicit or implicit rejection, their intimacy inhibited, and their personality thwarted because of parental and social prejudice; they become introverted and develop a sense of shame that may be compensated for by artistic or religious pursuits.[5] Oscar's choice of profession, his identification with his mother, his lack of identification with his father shown in rejecting his wishes, his exclusion of women from childhood games, his staying away from boys' sports and games, and his sensitive, reclusive personality suggest that he may have had an inclination to homosexuality, instilled by his upbringing, perhaps his constitution, or both. I found no evidence, however, of any practice of homosexuality in Oscar's reported behavior.

Oscar's compliant and submissive personality, his sensitivity and attention to detail, and his delicate constitution may have contributed to his early success in the same-sex environment of the priesthood. Once in seminary, Oscar became a star. Not only was he pious, intelligent, and obedient, but he was also nice looking, not in an athletic way but because of his pleasant appearance. He was also fairly light-skinned, which in the racist Salvadoran environment made him even more attractive.

Oscar's good looks and eagerness to please undoubtedly contributed to his success in the ecclesiastical world and to the meteoric ascent that was going to take him to the highest religious office in the country. There were no cardinals in El Salvador; the archbishop of San Salvador was at the top of the hierarchical ladder. As per Vatican tradition only archbishops of the See of Guatemala, the former capital of Central America, were appointed cardinals. El Salvador has a cardinal now but his role is mostly symbolic; the archbishop is still solidly in charge. Oscar was destined for greater things; he was selected to go to Rome and study at the top institution of higher Catholic learning: the Pontifical Gregorian University.

His shyness was proverbial. He has been described as alienated from the younger priests. It is possible that he felt uncomfortable with younger men. We do not know how he felt about women in those years, particularly given that he did not seem to have much contact with them, but in his later years, instead of looking for a place to reside in a male religious community, he lived in a community of nuns. The mother superior of the Carmelite religious women at the hospital of the Divine Providence, where he resided, told me that they were all a big happy family and that Romero relaxed in their company and enjoyed joking with them.

We know of very few close male friends in his relatively long life and career, but he remained close to his mother until she died. When he was appointed to work in San Miguel, where he stayed for almost three decades, she moved with him to a neighborhood in the same small provincial city. In spite of his busy schedule, he visited her daily until the day she died.[6] Most of his benefactors were women, sometimes belonging to the upper class, who helped him generously in his charitable undertakings.

One of Oscar's close male friends was Alfonso Valladares, his classmate in the San Miguel seminary who was also sent to Rome, where Romero joined him later. Valladares was extroverted and carefree just as much as Romero was introverted and obsessive. Unfortunately, Valladares died an early death. Another close friend was Jesuit Father Rutilio Grande, whose assassination affected Oscar deeply; the third was Mr. Salvador Barraza, an independent businessman who acted as his chauffeur and traveling companion. Upon close examination, other people mentioned as "friends" by the various biographers turn out to be acquaintances who had him over for lunch and were objects of his pastoral solicitude. His friendship with Barraza was very tender and close, to the point that people assumed they were related. It was not, however, a relationship among equals. Barraza was afraid of Romero's temper and bent over backward to accommodate his requests.

The two men traveled numerous times to Mexico and Guatemala. Twenty years after Romero's death, Barraza could still recollect minute details of their final trip to Guatemala. He remembers how Romero scratched his face on a tree branch when they were hiking together, and how they sneaked out to have a beer without being detected by the nuns with whom they were staying. He showed me the pictures of their trip to Mexico, one shot of them watching a circus show together and a rare picture of Romero in layman's clothing. Quite often, Barraza took him to the beach, scarcely thirty minutes away from San Salvador, where they relaxed together. This is what Romero did in the company of other priests on the morning of the day he was murdered.

That fateful day Barraza insisted on accompanying him to the Mass he was going to celebrate at the hospital for cancer patients, which turned out to be his last. According to

Barraza, Romero, out of a presentiment that something might happen, insisted that Barraza not go, thus possibly saving his friend's life. Barraza was one of the first persons to rush to the hospital when Romero was shot and was allowed to observe the autopsy that was performed. He told me how awful it was to watch his beloved friend and avatar being disemboweled and cut into pieces.

His closeness to Barraza points to the fact that the archbishop was able to find great enjoyment and satisfaction in his close relation to another man. As far as I was able to ascertain, he never quite did the same with a woman, partly, at least, because of his reservations about doing anything that may endanger his vow.

I have not been able to ascertain as many details of Romero's actual relationship with Rutilio Grande. It is highly significant that, to all appearances, the loss of this dear friend served as the catalyst that brought about the obvious change in the focus and orientation of his ministry. All those present at the moment Romero witnessed the death of his friend were impressed by the quality of grief evidenced by the archbishop in the face of such momentous loss.

His consternation was evident when he invited all those present to celebrate a Eucharist to commemorate Rutilio at the site of the crime. Prayer, liturgical or private, was the way in which he dealt with trying circumstances and conflicting feelings, but it is safe to assume that the depth of his affection for Rutilio was largely responsible for his extraordinary transformation. Most of his confreres argue that Romero's prophetic ministry was the natural outgrowth of his faithfulness to basic gospel values and Catholic doctrine, but no one denies the obvious correlation to the fact that he changed significantly, one may even say qualitatively, around the time of his friend's death. He may have also been motivated by feelings of intense guilt since he had told Rutilio to continue his ministry in the face of imminent danger; as his bishop he should have protected him. Essentially, he may have felt that he caused his best friend's death by underestimating the impending terror.

Rutilio was a mirror image of Romero. They were both afflicted with an obsessive-compulsive disorder manifested as serious scruples—Rutilio to the point that he was close to rejecting ordination because he felt unworthy and, for the same reason, tried to abandon the priesthood. Monseñor agonized over his performance in several areas, as well as over the fact that he had undertaken the vow of celibacy without sufficient reflection and maturity. Sexual preoccupations were not beyond the man who was regarded as chastely angelic.

Brockman says that Romero's emotional distress took him to therapy and that he even had to take time away to undergo a period of intensive psychoanalysis. He was diagnosed as an "obsessive compulsive perfectionist."[7] Significantly, Oscar's psychologist in El Salvador was murdered in his own home for unknown motives. It definitely seems as if someone was trying to cover up a sensitive revelation about the man who had already become an icon for the liberation movement. We will never know the secret Dr. Semsch took with him to the grave. His assassination became another one of the many crimes in

Salvadoran history that have never been solved or properly investigated. Possibly because of the stigma associated with talking to a mental health professional, Romero denied that he was seeking professional help with Dr. Semsch and maintained that he only talked to the doctor as a friend. However, they used to keep scheduled appointments. Barraza told me that he drove him to the psychologist's office regularly. Dr. Semsch abided by strict confidentiality regarding the content of his sessions with Romero.

It is important to note that chastity was one of the main areas of concern for Oscar. Contrary to the way it is, at times, with other priests, there are no confirmed rumors about Romero having affairs with women or having any children out of wedlock. It appears that he was very faithful to his vow of celibacy. At any rate, unlike some other priests or people who seem well suited for abstinence, celibacy was a real struggle for him—a vow he had to undertake consciously and laboriously.

I mentioned above the kind of ascetic training focused on the mortification of the flesh that Romero underwent in seminary such as the use of *cilicio* wire and flagellation. Another training device was the Spiritual Exercises, a very intensive prayer and meditation method based on Ignatius of Loyola's directives. After considering the horrors of hell, seminarians were made to feel that the salvation of one's self and other people's souls was directly related to the *minutest* details of one's performance and discipline. One of the more terrifying aspects of this suggestion was the way the retreat master drove home the idea that hell is eternal. This was the stuff our worst nightmares were made of. It was the kind of religious brain-washing that fed any propensity to the obsessive-compulsive behavior, displayed by both Rutilio and Romero. In religious parlance this is known as scruples. Dr. Semsch diagnosed it accordingly. It has been observed that a person with a consti-tutional inclination to obsessive-compulsive behavior may be attracted to the kind of institution that fosters such behavior.[8]

In the case of Romero, his humanity came through par-ticularly in the real fear he experienced regarding death and torture. Mother Luz Cuevas,[9] a nun who worked at the cancer hospital, told me how the archbishop used to stay awake at night in a hyper-vigilant state listening to the noises that per-haps indicated the approach of his killers. He willingly placed himself in the kind of situation where martyrdom was a likely outcome. He was also plagued by depression and obsessive-compulsive behavior. However, as noted before, none of the above implies moral failure. It is possible to say that at an unconscious level, martyrdom, no matter how sublime or jus-tifiable its context, may also be an expression of Thanatos and a fundamentally masochistic[10] act that is seen more as a rebirth than as an absolute extinction.

Unconscious motivations need not taint the martyr's merit or achievement. We are all subject to Thanatos and, as long as Eros or the life instinct predominates, we stay alive; neverthe-less, Thanatos is built into our psychology and even our physi-ology. Autoimmunity, or the drive toward death, is inscribed in our bodies since we are subject to extinction. From the moment we are born our cells begin to deteriorate, and basically it is the process in the organism to turn against its healthy cells, so that if we do not die from a disease we will eventually die from old age; ultimately, we are all destined to surrender. Individuals like Romero, who was willing to offer his life for the sake of his beliefs, may harbor a particularly intense form of this drive. Then it becomes love, actualized through self-sacrifice.

Mary Jones has disproved Freud's dictum that the Irish cannot be psychoanalyzed by giving us an illustration of the positive role of Thanatos in her analysis of James Joyce's "The Dead."[11] In the course of an evening party, which Joyce situates at the eve of the Feast of the Epiphany, the main character Gabriel, a cowardly man who lives his life in compliance with conventional rules and tries to please everyone, discovers that his life has been a sham. By talking to his wife Gretta about her former boyfriend Michael—whose name evokes rivalry because it is the name of another archangel—he comes to have an epiphany. He discovers that Michael died of consumption after waiting for Gretta in the rain when she was being taken to a convent. Suddenly it dawns on him that by his self-sacrifice—by giving in to Thanatos when Eros was no longer a possibility—Michael actualized true love and became an authentic human being. Both Eros and Thanatos are two sides of the same coin and can both be an expression of love. This realization becomes a liberating experience for a man who had been enslaved by a futile search for erotic satisfaction and was losing his soul in the process.

Jean-Paul Sartre developed a similar argument in his oeuvre Existential Psychoanalysis.[12] The human being *is* only at the moment of death. This is the defining moment. The rest is only *becoming* or existence. The hero of *Les Chemins de la Liberte* (*The Roads to Freedom*) was a coward that redeems himself by a heroic act at the moment of his death. Sartre's concept has far-reaching implications in discerning whether the individual is determined by forces he is neither aware of nor has control over. Sartre himself seemed prey to voluntarism in *Being and Nothingness*, in which the *etre pour-soi* (the for-itself) could almost be construed as a totally free agent. In the *Critique de la Raison Dialectique* he seemed to lean in the direction of structuralism when the totalizing agent was practically swallowed up in the "plurality of agencies" under the shadow of the dominant mode of production. The "universal singular" comes as close as possible to restoring some balance to the equation. There is still "the irreducible," that which no person or theory can explain and is totally different for everyone, but the determining power of other forces is given some due. According to Sartre, Romero would have become himself in his consciously accepting the risk of death by defying a merciless regime and following through with his decision until the end.

Peterson[13] points out that in spite of the many priests, religious, and laypeople killed in El Salvador for defending human rights, the only person Pope John Paul II referred to as a martyr was Oscar Romero. The classical concept of the martyr as one who dies to witness to the Christian faith becomes problematic when applied to Romero, because his concept of the Church was very broad to the point that it encompassed the entire Salvadoran people. The concept has been expanded to declare Romero a "martyr of charity," as in the case of Maximilian Kolbe, the Franciscan priest who offered his life to the Nazis in exchange for another prisoner. Thus, a martyr of charity is one who dies to actualize the central Christian tenet of love. Jon Sobrino has taken this analysis a little further to say that Romero was a "political martyr"—one who died for a popular cause. There is no precedent of any such canonization in Rome. In this work's postscript, I will expand on Romero's subsequent apotheosis, his canonization and the way in which it became possible in spite of serious conservative opposition.

At any rate, the amount of aggression that Romero endured and he himself manifested was substantial. We have to ask if this same kind of aggression did not generate, or at least nourish, his readiness for martyrdom. It is suggested in the title of a compilation of Romero's dictum, *The Violence of Love*.[14] It would seem as if, according to the gospel dictum, Romero found his life by losing it.

The identity crisis that plagued Romero for most of his life seemed to dissipate when he assumed his new role as the champion of the poor and the denouncer of injustice. His obsessive-compulsive behavior seemed to diminish considerably, and he acted as if he had found a clear sense of purpose. He was decisive and bold where before he had been timid and conciliatory. The shy cleric became transfigured at the pulpit; his sermons were clear and powerful, to the point that their broadcasts became number one in national ratings, even more popular than soccer games. His activist political and theological or, if you wish, ideological, transformation was also a flight into integration and health.

In a previous chapter I have described the image he used when admonishing the wealthy to give up their attachment to riches, to give up their rings—that is their wealth—lest their hands be cut off. As noted above this could be construed as an image of castration. Statements of that sort need to be taken into account. We have to ask if this kind of image did not stem from Romero's own feelings of castration as a man constrained to remain celibate, and, in spite of his powerful activism, impotent to stop the tide of injustice and violence sweeping Salvadoran society. His last homily was a clear demonstration of this when he begged and finally ordered the troops to stop the killing and repression. The day after the sermon he became their next victim.

It clearly follows that Romero harbored a great deal of anger—righteous, if you wish—due to the cruelty and severity of the repression that was unleashed on his Church and his people. His expressions of indignation echo those of the prophets of Israel like Amos, Jeremiah, and Isaiah, and were thoroughly justified. A Salvadoran priest told me that in the case of Romero, God's grace had totally taken over and his humanity had completely disappeared. This would run contrary to orthodox Christian theology that affirms in Jesus's Incarnation that God acts through human agency. Christian theology is eminently *incarnational,* in the sense that it calls for adherence to the principle that the Divine acts through historical circumstances and divine grace subsumes, but does not annihilate, humanity and freedom.

To acknowledge Romero's foibles and personal difficulties brings him closer to us as a model for emulation. It is not a matter of pathology versus grace, but rather, as Erikson pointed out in Luther's case, God's grace can and does act in us in spite of, and even through, our pathology. The same can be said in terms of a physical ailment; it can also be an instrument of the ultimate, as when a serious illness brings us into contact with lost or previously undiscovered spiritual dimensions. Romero's obsession with doing the right thing in the best possible way turned his traditional Catholic asceticism into a total dedication to the cause of justice and mercy.

Romero's homilies were his primary means of communication, particularly because they were broadcast nationally. Even the poorest of peasants had access to a transistor radio and could listen to his message. Through those broadcasts, he was transformed from a quiet clergyman into a roaring lion. He seemed to go into a trance when preaching, to the point that some eyewitnesses claim that it was literally an epiphany because his face shone when he delivered his sermons. His homilies were long (one and a half, sometimes close to two hours, made even longer by people interrupting often with applause). They were a mixture of journalistic report and theological excursus.

There was one theme that characterized his homilies: his unrelenting focus on the rich and his powerful and consistent denunciation of the injustices they committed against the poor. This is consistent with the traditions of the prophets of Israel, but it is harder to reconcile with Jesus of Nazareth's message of universal love, forgiveness, and forbearance. The latter, however, did not shy from his prophetic mission either and foresaw the deadly opposition his followers would endure, and the forceful resolution that would be necessary to follow him: "from the days of John the Baptist until now the kingdom of heaven suffereth violence, and the violent take it by force."[15]

There are basically two ways in which we can manifest aggression: turn it against ourselves or turn it against others. In the former case depression may ensue, to the point of suicidal ideation and actual attempts at suicide, while in the latter aggression is projected outwardly and directed toward others. The perceived wrongdoers are singled out as inimical to the point where nuances disappear and reality becomes increasingly black and white. In the case of Romero depression and symptoms of OCD gave way to his becoming intensely militant against the people responsible for the repressive atrocities.

It is quite evident that in his position as archbishop, Romero felt heavily charged with the lot of the Salvadoran people *in general*, not just for his Catholic fold. One has to wonder if the burden of grief and indignation did not become too hard for him to bear. We know that he was offered protection to safeguard him from attacks and that he refused to accept it. Perhaps at some point martyrdom appeared as a desirable option, not just because Catholic doctrine exalted it, but also because he was overwhelmed with the burden of his perceived responsibility. The absence of the usual consolation and support granted to other human beings—such as the companionship of a partner or spouse and the intimate circle of immediate family—may have been another factor in making his load even harder to bear. We must also keep in mind that not only his friend Rutilio but also several other priests had been assassinated, which may have caused him to experience survivor's guilt. But above all he may have coveted martyrdom because, at some level, it appeared to him as the ultimate realization of love. And this is indeed how it was received by the people he loved.

To sum it all up: Oscar Romero was a shy, compliant, conflicted individual who suffered from OCD, went through periods of incapacitating depression and exhaustion, and who was unsure about his decision to take the vow of celibacy. He was thrust into a position of great authority in an extremely violent and convulsed social situation, and he was confronted by the aggressive, articulate, and self-assured circle of priests and religious he inherited in the archdiocese. His strong religious and spiritual formation provided the basis for the new and persuasive interpretation of the gospel that was being presented to him as the one true forgotten message of Jesus Christ: liberation theology. Gustavo Gutiérrez's opus magna *A Theology of Liberation* had already been published and followed by an eruption of works from theologians all over the continent. He was in close contact with Jon Sobrino and Ignacio Ellacuria, two of the most renowned liberation theologians.

We have seen how he clung to what he saw as the truth with passionate conviction, even to the point of scruples, like when he adhered to traditional Vatican teaching and castigated his confreres for what he saw as their laxity in observance. This intensity and conviction now became directed against the constituted civil authorities whom he saw as illegitimate, or at least abusive of their power, and in the process subtler distinctions became blurred, practically nonexistent. He made occasional condemnations of leftist violence but they are few and far between and pale in comparison with his consistent attacks on official violence. Just as before he had ignored the appeals of the most liberal and progressive elements, in his later years he went against the advice and thinking of his brother bishops and was left practically alone in his unrelenting support for the left (Bishop Rivera y Damas, the only other prelate to take his side, was an auxiliary not a diocesan bishop).

Perhaps it takes this kind of personality to make a true prophet. The same fervor that prompted him to cling tenaciously to traditional Church doctrine was transferred to the liberation movement. It is as if, when we begin to entertain subtleties, we become mired in distinctions that make it difficult, if not impossible, to act with the conviction of an Oscar Romero. The legacy of Romero is clear when it comes to his ethical and moral stature, but it is not too clear when it comes to the overall effect it had in either preventing or unleashing the civil war that took the lives of seventy-five thousand Salvadorans, not counting the myriads disappeared, and that produced meager, or negative, results in terms of real change. ARENA (the Nationalist Republican Alliance), the party that founded the infamous death squads and was responsible for most of the repressive violence, remained in power at the end of the civil war. The FMLN (Farabundo Marti National Liberation Front) party that was born of the guerrilla organizations was found guilty of corruption and mismanagement and suffered a landslide loss in the 2019 presidential elections. The conditions of misery, illiteracy, unemployment, and disease remain unabated and are now compounded by widespread delinquency. The abysmal differences between social classes continue and have created a hyper security-conscious environment. Most businesses and establishments feature guards armed with semiautomatic weapons. The American embassy looms large in major public decisions.

We are left to wonder what could have possibly happened if Romero had adopted a stronger role as a mediator and been able to broaden his appeal to progressive elements among the middle and upper classes. He was clearly not a pacifist in the tradition of Mahatma Gandhi or Martin Luther King. According to Peterson, Romero's formulations and interpretation of the "just war" theory went beyond what is admissible in official Catholic doctrine, including the *Populorum Progressio* encyclical that Romero uses to substantiate his position on the matter. One of the preconditions laid out by Romero for the taking up of arms was that defensive violence can only be justified when it does not "bring in retaliation an even greater evil than is being resisted."[16]

There is no way to know in advance what the consequences of a rebellion may be. The correlation of forces, however, was not clear from the very beginning, and when the Soviet and Cuban assistance was withdrawn there was no way the rebel forces could take power; even if they were so to take it, there was no way to foresee or guarantee what would come of it.

I can understand and empathize with Romero's reaction. I was also nourished by the liberation theology movement and was active in Salvadoran politics both before and after I immigrated to the United States. Given the intensive climate of institutional and armed violence, and the consensus among progressive people regarding the futility of non-violent resistance, there appeared to be no other alternative than armed revolution. I believe if I had stayed in El Salvador I would have actively joined the opposition and perhaps followed the same lot as Romero and other martyred priests whom I met as fellow seminarians: Octavio Ortiz, Ernesto Barrera, Alfonso Navarro, and Alirio Napoleon Macias, as well as my Jesuit mentors. When I speak about survivor's guilt I do so from the standpoint of my personal experience. While in the United States, I joined the movement to denounce the situation of El Salvador and made a tour of Europe to collect funds and support for the popular church. I even made an attempt to return during the war. I was advised by my companions in the struggle to remain overseas where I could be more useful. Still, sometimes I experience the gnawing feeling of guilt over the mere fact of being alive.

This is not the place to detail the legacy of the war, or to speculate what would have been the result of a sustained pacifist approach to the crisis in El Salvador. That would take another study altogether, one of monumental proportions. But it does appear that the unleashing of the Salvadoran civil war was the result of a tragic miscalculation that led to unprecedented carnage and plunged the country into chaos.

There has been no direct correlation established between Romero's assassination and the outbreak of the Salvadoran civil war, but it does seem evident that his murder was the catalyst for the outbreak of open hostilities on the rebel's side. The conflict had been in the making for a long time. The Salvadoran left enjoyed the support of the former Soviet Union via Cuba and the tiny country of El Salvador became a pawn in the grander geopolitical struggle. El Salvador is still afflicted by lack of infrastructure and numerous social ills that appear to be a sequel of the armed conflict. However, the purpose of this case study has been to contribute to the understanding of the personality of one of the most significant figures of the twentieth century, and how the interaction between this kind of person and his historical context produced the prophetic phenomenon we know as Archbishop Oscar Romero.

This work's findings may be summarized as follows:

Romero was born to a modest family of small landowners who became dispossessed by unjust means, which left an imprint on young Oscar that sensitized him to the plight of the poor.

He was drawn to his mother's interests, rather than his father's, and chose a profession that imposed restrictions on his sexuality. The boy's constitution, coupled with his father's rejection and alcoholism, caused him a great deal of conflict manifested in interpersonal difficulties, depression, and obsessive-compulsive behavior.

Liberation theology and his elevation as archbishop provided an opportunity for formerly repressed or suppressed
impulses to be manifested in vigorously attacking systemic
injustice and being placed at the pinnacle of the opposition's
leadership.

The anger and guilt generated by the death of coworkers and friends may have contributed to a death wish manifested in his willingness to actualize the ideal of martyrdom
promoted by Catholic doctrine and tradition. However, his
radical and final choice facilitated a flight into health that dis-
sipated the archbishop's psychological ailments and became a
self-realization of his true self in Christ.[17]

When I was a student at EDS in Cambridge I met Bishop
Dom Helder Camara and celebrated a Eucharist with him. At
the time of the consecration he went into a trance and it was
clear he was seeing *something* the rest of us could not. It was
a mystical trance and it looked like it was going to be harder
for him to conclude the Mass. There was a dialogue in lieu of
a sermon, with questions and answers. Somebody asked about
Romero and he went into a trance of pure joy. He spoke about
the incomparable blessing of offering one's live to Christ and
said he was envious of Romero for the opportunity he had been
granted to die for the Lord. Bishop Camara had been threat-
ened many times and he seemed like he was, not just ready, but
anxious to make the same offering.

The above-mentioned factors help us understand why
Romero chose a very antagonistic approach to the sectors
deemed responsible for the crisis in El Salvador. It is difficult

to conceive that a man with Romero's background could have done anything different, but in the end, he did not have to, he could have continued in his former path. We are left with the irreducible: an individual's choice in the face of a myriad of conditioning, and sometimes strongly conflicting, factors.

CHAPTER 5

FINDING RESONANCE

Even though the focus of a psychobiography is the subject under scrutiny, a psychoanalytically oriented work cannot ignore the emotional responses and perceptions elicited in the author. Throughout the case study the words and deeds of Romero resonated within me and prompted a series of reflections and responses that, in my opinion, will contribute to enrich this work. This kind of feedback may be similar to what in psychoanalytic parlance is known as "countertransference."[1] The reader's impressions are bound to be valuable in terms of gauging the effect the subject had, and still has, on others.

There were other impressions when visiting the crypt in the basement of the cathedral where Romero is buried, but even more so in the chapel at the cancer hospital where he was killed—a strong sense of the supernatural. The first time I visited the chapel I sensed a strong smell of blood that was not offensive, but on the contrary was pleasant and unearthly, like some delicate perfume; I felt the presence of holiness. Call it autosuggestion or a psychological phenomenon, if you wish, but it was very real to me.

I met Oscar A. Romero in 1970 when he was fifty-three years old. Monsignor Luis Chavez y Gonzalez was then archbishop of San Salvador, and Romero was the auxiliary bishop of San Salvador. I was a twenty-four-year-old in search of an answer to the quandary of life, and a member of the Christian Student Movement. The archbishop had placed Monsignor Romero in charge of a campaign led by a North American priest, Father Patrick Peyton, to promote the daily praying of the Rosary among Salvadoran families. Father Patrick Peyton was a powerful personality. He was born January 9, 1909, in Ireland. He was a member of a family of nine children. At the age of nineteen he and his brother Tom immigrated to the United States to join their sister Nellie. His wish from boyhood was to be ordained a priest but his family in Ireland was unable to meet the cost of his education. In the United States he returned to full-time education and studied for the priesthood. During his final year in the seminary he was diagnosed as having tuberculosis. At that time tuberculosis was incurable. Fr Patrick was very weak and was given little hope by the medical team of recovering to full health, but he had great faith and prayed to the Blessed Virgin Mary for a recovery to health. His prayers were answered and his health began to improve, to the amazement of the medical profession. He was ordained to the priesthood on June 15, 1941. Father Peyton was so grateful to the Blessed Virgin Mary for his health that he, with the permission of his superiors, began the prayer crusade, which took him all over the world preaching the importance of prayer, especially family prayer. He staged hundreds of radio and television shows with many of the famous movie stars of Broadway and Hollywood taking part. He was the founder of "Family Rosary" and "Family Theatre."

Because of the generalized poverty and social disintegration, compounded by alcoholism, in the Central American region, the structure of the Salvadoran family is predominantly matriarchal. The majority of children grow up in single-mother families. This has given rise to the cult of women known as *Marianism*: the exaggerated veneration of women and the glorification of the pain, hardship, and suffering they must undergo to raise their offspring. The Church's strategy with the Rosary campaign was to appeal to the religious sentiments of the population to persuade them to stay together, through thick and thin, without addressing the socioeconomic root causes of family disintegration.

At that time the influence of liberation theology had begun to be felt. We university students protested against the Rosary campaign because we considered it too conservative. The campaign's slogan was "The Family that Prays Together Stays Together." Our counter slogan was "The Family that *Eats* Together Stays Together." To us, a campaign to promote prayer in a country ravaged by family and generalized hunger and an endless succession of military dictatorships seemed at best ludicrous if not perverse. However, because of my conservative background and the exposure that the opportunity afforded, I agreed to appear at a rally for the Rosary campaign, praying the Rosary in public. The massive gathering took place in front of the Church of the Holy Rosary, located in Plaza Libertad (Freedom Plaza) in downtown San Salvador. Peasants were transported in buses and trucks from their remote hamlets and villages to attend the event. Plaza Libertad has been the scene of numerous marches and rallies against the government in El Salvador's tumultuous history.

Fifty years later, I still have a vivid recollection of that day. Bishop Romero stood next to us but said nothing. He was a quiet, unpretentious man, and, at the time not generally known as an eloquent preacher or dynamic leader. At this event, he was simply a figurehead who, because of his hierarchical position, lent prestige and authority to the event. He was then considered the epitome of all things conservative and an outright enemy of the progressive forces. Father Ramon Carramolinos, the priest who persuaded us to appear at the event, was far more charismatic. He told us that we could use the campaign as a means to gather people and teach them liberation theology. In this way we would subvert the campaign's conservative bent by instructing the people in a new way to interpret the gospel. Whereas Romero was shy and hermetic, Carramolinos was exuberant and gregarious. He was up to date with the latest theological currents emanating from Europe and South America and was very open with us about things such as his difficulty in keeping the vow of celibacy. During my last visit to El Salvador I was told that he had married.[2]

As early as the 1960s the pressures of generalized poverty, political repression, and the concentration of power in the hands of a few pushed the Catholic Church to define itself vis â vis the status quo. In 1968 the Latin American Bishops Conference (CELAM)[3] met in Medellin, Colombia, to discuss ways in which the innovations of the Second Vatican Council could be adapted to Latin America. It became a most revolutionary event that provided enormous impetus for the Church to become involved in social change because it declared that it was the Church's duty to act on behalf of the poor and the oppressed. This intensified divisions in the Church, which generally took place along class lines. Priests, nuns, religious, and laypeople who worked with the peasants and the urban poor followed the directives of Medellin, and the bishops and priests who served the wealthier classes took a stand against it.

I was never to see Romero again. I was awarded a scholarship to attend Baldwin-Wallace College in Berea, Ohio, and immigrated to the United States in 1973. I received the news of his death in 1980 when I was a student at the Episcopal Divinity School in Cambridge, Massachusetts. There, I was the main speaker in a massive rally to commemorate the martyrdom of a man who was by then well known as far away as Japan and who had become the symbol of the liberation church. Shortly afterward, the civil war erupted. I made an attempt to return and join the resistance, but my friends and companions in the struggle advised me to stay in the United States and work with the solidarity movement for the people of El Salvador. I also traveled through Europe on a speaking tour to publicize the plight of the Salvadoran people and collect funds for the liberation theology movement.

The archbishop's ministry had a direct influence on my future course. His assassination was a catalyst for the thirteen-year civil war that ravaged El Salvador. My prolonged stay in the US, occasioned by the war, led me to establish marriage and family commitments here and to become a US citizen. My ties to El Salvador, however, remained strong. The need to come to terms, intellectually and emotionally, with the period in Salvadoran history preceding and comprising the 1980s civil war became imperative to me.

I concluded that understanding the interface between Romero's personal life and his historical context and his transformation from conservative priest to radical archbishop was a crucial part of this endeavor. Perhaps I experienced a kind of survivor's guilt. Most of the native clergymen who were assassinated were classmates of mine at San Jose Seminary in San Salvador and the Jesuits Martin Baro, Segundo Montes, and Ignacio Ellacuria were my mentors and professors at the Catholic university.

I can personally identify with Romero's feelings, since my own experience parallels the archbishop's. I also grew up in a landowner middle-class Salvadoran family. My parents divorced when I was an infant. As in Romero's case my father suffered from alcoholism and I saw very little of him when I was a child. Like Romero, I also identified strongly with feminine figures since I grew up with my maternal grandparents and my mother. This was tempered, however, by the strong presence of my grandfathers, who were successful, kind, and attentive to my needs.

When I was a child, until I was eleven years old, my mother's family was quite well off. My grandfather owned land and a soap factory. But my grandfather was dispossessed of his land by a clever swindler and lost his factory because of illness. Like the Romeros, we found ourselves reduced to a very modest way of life.

I will never forget the day we had to move from a very comfortable house in the middle of town to a small place in the outskirts. As a result, I developed bitterness toward the indolent rich who flaunted their wealth in a country where the immense majority lacked the most basic necessities. The similarities end here because, unlike in Romero's case, one of the indolent rich was my own father who had managed to retain his business and his properties but did not contribute adequately to my rearing and support. In 1945 my father had managed to obtain a scholarship at Indiana State University in Fort Wayne that provided a program for an accelerated degree in civil engineering. Fort Wayne, Indiana, became the stuff of my most grand fantasies. Twenty-eight years later, while I was a student in Ohio, I drove through Fort Wayne and found it to be a pathetic small town, more like a strip of fast food chains and cheap motels. The college itself was not impressive. And this is what I had envied and resented so much. My own college, Baldwin-Wallace, was more distinguished. The image of my father, however, still loomed large because of his landed ruling class pedigree and financial success; although in literary and philosophical matters he was an ignoramus.

My father went through periods of intensive drinking to the point that he had to be hospitalized. But even during his periods of sobriety he ignored me. I hardly remember seeing him at all when I was a child. Perhaps the absence of a consistent father figure caused me to go through periods in which I was shy and compliant. But when the opportunity arose as a university student I became politically involved and vehemently opposed to the establishment. I also went through periods of depression and found it difficult to establish friendships. My father's absence weighed heavily on me. I see myself reflected in the retiring and reclusive personality of the archbishop as well as in his need to lash out.

It took me many years of intensive psychoanalysis to work through my need to smooth over troubles, my lack of assertiveness, and my difficulties in establishing relationships. Surely both Romero and I were justified in denouncing the blatant injustices of the period; in my case the anger was also definitely personal. It is likely that it was the same for Romero. In my opinion the personal aspect does not make it any less justified. Like the Romeros, my mother's family, with whom I lived, had been dispossessed by fraudulent means and my father abandoned me. My father's abandonment, however, was less definite and radical; he died when I was fifty-four years old, whereas Romero was orphaned as a teenager. And there is no abandonment worse than death.

Like Romero, I also experienced perfectionism, in particular when I was a Roman Catholic seminarian. I went through a period of scruples not unlike the kind of rigid adherence to rules that has been described of Romero. The emptiness I experienced as a result of the emotional and social chasm of my upbringing manifested itself in behaviors aimed at overcompensating. I strove to keep all the rules impeccably and to lead an intensive prayer life. This led to some teasing on the part of other seminarians and to jocular rumors that I was on my way to pursue sainthood.

There was an incident, however, that brought to light my repressed feelings of anger. We were having lunch at the refectory and one of my classmates was teasing me relentlessly. I continued to eat in silence until I finally lost my temper, jumped over the table and punched him in the face. No one teased me after that. The seminarian's name was Manuel Reyes. On October 7, 1980, scarcely six months after Romero's assassination, the tortured cadaver of Father Manuel Reyes was found on a country road. Like his bishop, he had been murdered for working with the poor. He was the first Salvadoran priest to follow Romero on the road to martyrdom since he was killed after the latter's murder. Seven had already preceded him. The veneer of saintliness I exhibited at the seminary seemed phony to me because I was unable to persevere in a life of self-denial; instead I came to the imperial metropolis to enjoy the privileges of American society, whereas Manuel laid down his life for his people. The testimony of Manuel, Romero, and all my former classmates who died in the struggle gave rise within me to considerable feelings of guilt, anger, and depression. I developed animadversion and even hatred toward all things Catholic and, like his confrères, I disliked Romero in particular. There was a part of me that admired his sacrifice but also a part that wanted to question it. That led me to explore whether Romero's sacrifice had not been perhaps motivated by his neurosis and by a kind of death drive. This is important to note as at times my guilt and anger have colored this work to the point that it may seem overly pessimistic and negative.

The similarities between Romero and me cannot be discounted. Later on, like Romero, I assumed the stance of the troublemaker challenging both ecclesiastical and political systems. I became involved in the liberation theology movement from its very inception and was a student leader at the Jesuit Catholic university. Had I not been awarded a scholarship to complete my higher education in the United States I would most likely have been killed also. Then I became critical of my new denomination and lashed out against what I perceived as their classist and racist attitudes. As a result of my outspoken criticism I remained marginal in the institutional Church for another ten years, working in the field of mental health.

During the 1980s I labored in the Dickensian atmosphere of homeless shelters in the Bronx and in Manhattan. During that time, I decided to undergo five times a week, on the couch, intensive psychoanalysis to explore the roots of my anger and depression. Although psychoanalysis has been submitted to heavy questioning in terms of its therapeutic efficacy, it was very helpful to me in terms of accepting the limitations inherent in the system and coming to terms with authority figures. Eventually, I was able to make a tenuous peace with the hierarchy and returned to fulltime ministry. When I began this book's work, I was the pastor of St. Mark's Church in-the-Bowery located in the East Village of Manhattan.

I went through the same cycle as Romero, from extreme compliance and institutional obeisance to outspoken challenge to the prevailing structures. In either case both adjustment and rebellion may have fit the same purposes, that is, either to compensate for the absence of a healthy, loving, and protective father figure, or to protest against the injustice of authority figures. What is most striking is how these two apparently totally opposite movements can stem from the same psychological roots and be displayed so prominently in the life of a single person.

Three years before Romero's arrival at the seminary in San Salvador I spent a year at the same place and became familiar with the juxtaposition of traditional and progressive theology espoused by the Jesuits. For instance, some would balk at the use of the *cilicio* while others recommended it wholeheartedly. My intensity in trying to abide by all the rules and commandments of the Catholic Church and to carry out the study and workload was so intense that I also became bothered with fatigue and scruples. My physician recommended that I take a year off. I was never to return to the seminary because of my involvement with lay ministries and an even clearer conviction that I was not called to undertake the vow of celibacy that is still mandatory for Roman Catholic clergy. Only the clergy of the Eastern Uniate churches in communion with Rome are exempted from the rule.[4]

Like Oscar I tried the use of the *cilicio*[5] but after a few times I decided it was not for me. I left the Roman Catholic seminary after one year. The pressure was too intense and was taking a toll on me. My doctor said I was exhausted. On the other hand, the book *Lay People in the Church* by Yves Congar had unleashed a veritable flurry of interest and passion for the ministry of the laity. At the time this was a revolutionary concept arising as a fruit of the Second Vatican Council. It provided an outlet for my desire to serve in the church. Congar, who was a Dominican monk, made a persuasive case for the relevance and equal standing of lay ministers. Shortly afterward, Jose Maria Escriva, the founder of the Opus Dei, was to refashion and promote Congar's ideas in a conservative fashion.

I was definitely not celibate material. I was very attracted to women and I envisioned myself as a father and husband. Later I was going to retake the priestly vocation in the Episcopal Church where I could actualize both.

I mentioned countertransference before because all throughout the writing and researching for this case study my feelings about Romero ran high. I became aware of it not only because of my own reflection, but also thanks to the observations of my dissertation committee. Ever since I left the Roman Catholic Church, I had experienced a kind of inferiority complex due to the fact that I had been heavily indoctrinated to believe that it was the only true church. I resented the arrogance of Catholic priests who acted as if they were holy and pure and, in fact, above we non-Roman Catholic clergy who are tainted by sex. Archbishop Chavez, Romero's predecessor, used to say that Catholic priests were "the princes of El Salvador"[6] and should behave as such. It was also common knowledge that many if not most of them had lovers, but they were very secretive and it was hard to tell who was keeping their vows. Subsequent scandals have exposed the culture of secrecy and the crimes and the hypocrisy of some Catholic clergy and yet they still project an image of superiority essentially based solely on their professed continence. Celibacy became the most distinguishing quality of Catholic clergy in the West and it was possibly Romero's greatest concern until he took up the cause of the poor.

Romero was for me the quintessential expression of the arrogance of the Roman clergy. And though I recognized the significance of his ministry I still harbored serious doubts about the involvement of his ego in the matter of his martyrdom. To be a martyr has been held as the highest virtue in the Catholic tradition and in laying down his life, or being willing to do it and flirting with danger, Romero became holy to a different constituency, just as before he had been considered a saint by abiding by the precepts of the institution. My dentist, who is solidly middle class, told me, "We are going to have a saint for half of the Salvadoran people."

I also became aware of survivor's guilt having to do with my own internalization of the ideal of martyrdom. I mentioned before how I had wanted to return to El Salvador and join the resistance because I felt that is what I *had* to do. But there was a part of me that did not want to take that risk. This felt to me as a deficiency on my part, even if consciously I was convinced that staying in the States was the best I could do.

Toward the end of this work I came to the conclusion that if I had been in Romero's position, I would have probably done the same, although I believe he and his image were seriously manipulated by the left and by the right. Theoretically, he could have still taken a different path, although it is hard to conceive given his sensitivity to the people's needs and the severe repression that had been unleashed against the church and the general population.

Most people I talked to and interviewed refused to admit that Romero had undergone a conversion in the traditional sense, that is a radical change of beliefs and attitudes. They saw the new direction of his ministry as a logical outcome of his Christian values and his desire to do always what was best. But it would take an immense degree of humility and holiness not to succumb to the glory of being, at one point, the most influential man in the country, whose fame extended well beyond its borders.

How much was motivated by narcissism and how much by selfless love no one can tell. These data belong to the hidden motivations that are simply not accessible. The ideal of martyrdom, however, particularly in a post-9-11 world remains open to question. Every time I return to El Salvador and witness the ongoing poverty and violence, now attributed to gangs and highway robbers, I think of how futile Romero's sacrifice seems to be. Many of the delinquents are believed to be former combatants unable to find employment. Perhaps the effects of Romero's ministry will not be perceived until some very distant future. A prophet, however, has to witness to the truth even if the people refuse to hear it.

POSTSCRIPT

The Apotheosis

The twenty-third of May, in the year of our Lord 2015, was one of the greatest days in the history of El Salvador: more than two hundred and fifty thousand people filled the streets of San Salvador to witness the outdoor ceremony of the beatification of Oscar Romero. Gigantic screens and loudspeakers had been placed on the street leading from the Metropolitan Cathedral to the site of the ceremony (a 5.9 km distance): the Monument to the Divine Savior, a fifty-nine-foot tower with the effigy of a triumphant Jesus on top. Most of the people in the crowd were workers and peasants who had arrived from every corner of the land. On a stage placed at the bottom of the monument were four presidents; the papal nuncio; the archbishop; and many dignitaries, including Roberto D'Aubuisson Arrieta, the major of Santa Tecla and the son of the culprit of Romero's assassination.

The canonization took place in Rome. The name "Romero" comes from Rome and it means "pilgrim going to Rome." Romero was a frequent visitor, he attended the Gregorian Seminary there, and, finally, it was there that his achievement was confirmed by the church who claimed him as its own. Some are uncomfortable with the title of "saint" because they think Romero does not fit the bill, but in many ways he does. He was a contemplative man of prayer and consciously practiced self-denial. As far as I was able to ascertain, he was also faithful to his vow of celibacy and, until the last three years of his life, like the ascetic hermits, he was shy of the public life.

Romero's canonization had been held up during the reign of Pope Jean Paul II, now also a saint, who was canonized shortly after his passing. Jean Paul II was an advocate of human rights and defender of the poor, but having lived in Poland most of his life he was highly suspicious of anything reeking of Marxism. There was also pressure from the right-wing Salvadoran government to stop it.

Romero had to wait until Joseph Ratzinger became Benedict XVI. The latter allowed the canonization process to continue, thus affirming the fact that his martyrdom, although not caused by explicitly confessing Jesus as the Christ, was in fact caused by his affirmation, unto death, of core Christian values in the face of crude despotism and atrocious wealth inequality. Pope Francis, more liberal than his predecessor, affirmed the process and expedited its completion.

Finally, Romero was canonized on October 14, 2018, after a miracle attributed to his intercession was confirmed. Three miracles were submitted to the Congregation for the Causes of Saints in Rome but, after an extensive investigation and documentation, they were rejected. A fourth one, however, was accepted. Cecilia Maribel Flores laid in a coma caused by a cesarean surgery; her husband prayed fervently to Blessed Oscar Romero, and she, against all medical expectations, came out of the coma. After this there were no more obstacles to his elevation to the altars. The Episcopal and Lutheran churches had already included him in their calendars. The ceremony took place this time in Rome, thirty-eight years after his martyrdom. Because of the country's poverty, not as many Salvadorans were able to attend; the ones who managed to make it were mostly clergy, religious orders, and middle-class Catholics. The human rights attorneys I interviewed were also in attendance.

Legal Proceedings

On March 6, 2020, I met with the director and the chief assistant prosecutors of the "Human Rights and Legal Protection Association Dr. Maria Julia Hernandez (*Asociacion de Derechos Humanos y Proteccion Legal Dra. Maria Julia Hernandez*)." The outfit is named after a prominent Catholic lawyer who was a vigorous defender of the victims of war in El Salvador. They are in charge of the investigation and eventual capture of the men involved in the killing of Romero. We sat in an open, spacious, second-floor office overlooking San Salvador's penitentiary, which is located across the street.

They related to me the existence of a cabal of businessmen, financiers, politicians, and mobsters known as "Grupo Miami," based in the city of the same name, who were the masterminds of the crime. The "Grupo" organized and created the infamous "death squads" responsible for innumerable crimes and disappearances. In them participated well-known members of the so-called *"buenas familias"* ("good families"); that is, the wealthiest Salvadoran upper crust.

Love of money, "which is a form of idolatry,"[1] was at the root of everything. That is what Romero denounced and that is why they decided to kill him. It is important to point out the racism prevalent in Salvadoran society. Given that most of the wealthy are of European descent, and either white or very light skinned, the rest, for them, is just a mass of expendable *"indios."*[2] That has been the case from colonial times up to the very present and was most evident in the massacre of 1932. The image below[3] is one of the numerous death threats sent to the archbishop and it clearly shows the right-wing nationalistic fascist convictions. There are fascistic groups in America also, but they have remained a fringe; in El Salvador they were the ruling class.

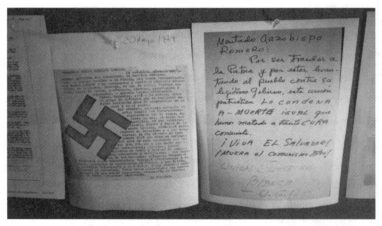

Copies of two death threats received by Monsignor Romero during his three years of archbishopric: one signed by the "Unión Guerrera Blanca" and the other signed by "La Falange."[4]

What the human rights lawyers described to me, in extensive detail, was a consistent and carefully calculated obstruction of justice. This was done by destroying evidence and preventing witnesses to testify, either by hiding, disappearing, or simply eliminating them.

For starters, Romero was killed with an explosive bullet that, although it left only a small entry wound, scattered dozens of pellets inside his body. All the pellets and the bullet *disappeared* after a complete autopsy, performed immediately after the shooting; therefore, it was impossible to identify the exact murder weapon.

The intellectual author of the crime, Roberto D'Aubuisson, died an ignominious and painful death from esophageal cancer and bleeding ulcers. It is ironic that the crime was committed at the chapel of the hospital for cancer patients where the archbishop resided.

Coincidentally, or perhaps providentially, two days after I met with the prosecutors the internet newspaper *elfaro.net* published an extensive interview with Captain Alvaro Saravia, one of the main culprits, who is still in hiding. After the crime, Saravia flew to Fresno, California, before he could be arrested. There, he worked as a pizza delivery man, used car salesman, and money launderer until he went underground to, according to the human rights lawyers, some remote place in Honduras. The location had to be kept confidential. Wherever that is, it must be someplace where most people are non-white because Saravia, being of fair complexion, is known there as "El Gringo" (The American).

Saravia's actual capture is now in the hands of Interpol. He is also wanted for migratory violations in the US, but the order of arrest for his participation in Romero's murder came from the Salvadoran attorney general. The Center for Justice and Accountability (CJA) also brought a civil suit, which resulted in his being ordered to pay $10,000,000 to Romero's relatives for his participation in the crime. Amado Garay, the driver who transported the sharpshooter, is in protective custody in the US. Five others who were identified as participants in the crime were not able to hide. One was decapitated, another committed suicide, another disappeared, another was killed at a highway checkpoint, and the fifth ended up torn to pieces. It seems as if we cannot rule out some kind of divine justice.

Saravia told the reporter an amazingly shocking story of drugs, women, and murder. The cadre got together in the house of Roberto "Bobby" Daglio, a wealthy Salvadoran businessman residing in Miami, Florida. Daglio and Saravia were both pilots, the latter was a captain in the Salvadoran air force. There, they engaged in orgies with an abundant supply of cocaine, whisky, and women. All the group members carried state-of-the-art guns, some even in ankle holsters. They plotted and carried out wild orgies there, caught up in a ferocious anticommunist fever. For them it was a matter of protecting the country from atheistic communism; nobody was safe and everyone was fair game. They would have made McCarthyism[5] look like a fairy tale.

The man who actually pulled the trigger has not been identified yet. Someone presented a sketch of a bearded man, but it could be anybody; it is not descriptive enough. In the interview, Saravia described how he kept careful notes of the weapons and vehicles needed for the operation and how it was carried out. Another wealthy businessman, Roberto Mathies Regalado, owner of the VW franchise in El Salvador, supplied the Passat that was used for the operation.

People in the highest societal circles were also implicated; among them Enrique Viera Altamirano, director of the major right-wing newspaper *El Diario de Hoy*, and a man whose last name was Muyshondt, possibly related to the current mayor of San Salvador.[6] The conspiracy came from the highest socio-economic circles. A Salvadoran professional, an ordinary *pater familias* who didn't know my leanings, confided to me that he would have killed Romero if only he had had a chance. As Jesuit priest and theologian Jon Sobrino once pointed out, "Telling the truth is the most dangerous thing."

When attending Romero's canonization in Rome Cardinal Gregorio Rosa Chavez, the highest prelate in El Salvador, asked for a speedy trial for the persons accused of Romero's murder. He said only justice can heal the wounds of the war, and accused the Salvadoran ambassadors in Rome of blocking Romero's canonization in order to protect Roberto D'Aubuisson, the founder of their party. Although most people identified as involved in the killing have perished, there are still some at large, among them the man who pulled the trigger.

Other persons implicated are Mario Ernesto Molina Contreras and Pedro Lobo; the former was the son of President Colonel Arturo Armando Molina, a powerful president who ruled El Salvador from 1972 to 1977. Mario has been described as a brat who was born with a silver spoon in his mouth and had access to money, power, and privilege. He saw himself as a member of a military-governmental aristocracy that basically provided him with impunity. The former, Pedro Lobo, allegedly—most likely under duress—confessed to his participation in the crime. The video of the confession was shown on TV channels 2 and 6 and caused a sensation but a judge confiscated the video which was then mysteriously lost.

In his father's presidential palace Molina met Saravia and D'Aubuisson. The palace guards became Mario's security detail; one of those men was the sniper who ended the archbishop's life. But because of persistent obstructions, such as losing evidence and disappearing witnesses, the name of the shooter remains undisclosed. Mario Molina disappeared. It is rumored he is somewhere in the United States.

The greatest enigma continues to be the identity of the man who pulled the trigger. An odontologist called Tito Regalado was implicated but this has not been verified. The car used for the killing was taken to a junkyard and totally destroyed; no license plates were ever identified. One of the saddest things of the entire tragedy was that the shooter was paid a measly 1,000 Salvadoran *colones* for the murder, which translates into $114.40 when converted into US dollars. One hundred and fourteen dollars and forty cents, instead of 30 shekels, was all it took to eliminate one of the greatest figures of the twentieth century.

The Sequel

It has been argued that Romero's killing was the trigger that caused the people to rise, but that is quite debatable. The war was bound to explode. The government's repression had reached intolerable levels; the war had been brewing since colonial times. As mentioned before, the theft of indigenous communal lands and the grossly unequal distribution of wealth, made greatly worse by the despotism of the armed forces and their ruling class, were the main factors in unleashing the armed conflict. To these local factors we must add the geopolitical fact that the region had become the grounds where the US and the Soviet Union were fighting for hegemony.

The war was a catastrophic mistake. More than seventy-five thousand people died and an unknown number disappeared. The war provoked a massive immigration to the United States and gave rise to the infamous *maras*, or gangs, which originated in LA and subsequently returned to become the new repressive and terrorizing factor in Salvadoran society. Schafik Handal, the main communist leader, has been quoted as saying that the war caused the development of the country to suffer at least a fifty-year setback.

The collapse of the Soviet Union, which provided the main support to the guerrillas, forced the latter to negotiate. Twenty years later the political party formed by the former guerrillas finally won the elections but ended up causing widespread disappointment by becoming like its right-wing predecessors. No structural change was implemented, the oligarchy continued to rule, living like kings in an island of misery. The Salvadorans forgot Chairman Mao's warning about not starting a war unless you were sure you were going to win it.

In addition, Mauricio Funes, the first leftist president, is a fugitive accused of embezzling $351 million, a sum equivalent to almost one and a half times the national GDP. That, in a country ravaged by 65 percent unemployment or underemployment and lack of adequate housing, health care, and education. After all the suffering and death it took to bring them to power, the leftist party ended up sorely disappointing the people and suffered a devastating defeat in the last presidential elections—from which, most likely, it will never recover.

Prophecy

The role of the prophet is not about productivity and effectiveness; rarely, if ever, does the prophecy yield the desired results and often in the end leads to the death of the messenger who brings what many consider to be bad news. This applied also to Jesus. In fact, the prophet brings good news to those who are willing to receive it and to change. Yet this is extremely difficult, almost a miracle, to those of us who are ensnared in the worship of comfort and wealth. It is "easier for a camel to pass through the eye of a needle."[7] It is indeed very difficult but not impossible; nothing is impossible for God.

Beginning with Zacchaeus and Matthew who were tax collectors, all the way to Francis of Assisi and Dulce Lopez Pontes in Brazil, Louis IX, Hedwig and Hermenegild, kings and queens have given up their treasure for the sake of the kingdom of heaven. It all hinges on encountering Jesus, and realizing that what he offers is the lost coin, the pearl of great price, the treasure buried in a field—something so big and final that, in encountering it, a person leaves everything else to achieve that prize. This, however, presupposes entering a different dimension. At first, the disciples didn't understand it. Even death becomes irrelevant in comparison with God's gift, and the attachment to this world is revealed as vacuous. The cross is still a stumbling block for the Jews and nonsense for us Gentiles.[8]

"Money is like manure," Thornton Wilder once said. "It's not worth a thing unless it's spread around encouraging young things to grow." And William James, in a letter written to H. G. Wells on September 11, 1906, said that "the moral flabbiness born of the exclusive worship of the bitch-goddess SUCCESS. That—with the squalid cash interpretation put on the word 'success'—is our national disease." No tweaking can do it; structural change, born of a profound personal and societal spiritual transformation, is needed.

We are living in a world where fabulous wealth is increasingly concentrated in the hands of a few. At the time of this writing a pandemic of an extremely contagious virus (COVID-19) has been unleashed on the world's population; but we have a more permanent and malignant plague, it is called poverty. The facts about world poverty are most alarming. One third of all deaths are caused by poverty. It is estimated that eighteen million people a year die from it; approximately six hundred million children live in dire poverty and execrable conditions. More than ten million children die of hunger and preventable diseases; it is a permanent pandemic caused simply by greed and exploitation. We have become very good at jumping on the bandwagon of relatively safe cultural issues, but remain silent when our personal security is at stake.

Mammon (money) was Jesus's archenemy and still is. Presently, it has been enthroned as a god by *consumerism*, which has now become a world religion. This is what Romero fought against; not out of Marxist convictions, but because he possessed deeply held convictions about his duty as a Christian. He did it knowing that his death was the price, and accepted it as God's will for standing up on behalf of the poor. Only somebody possessed by God's Sprit could do this. When he preached, he transformed from a rather misanthropic and small man into a roaring lion!

"Very truly I tell you, unless a grain of wheat falls to the ground and dies, it remains only a single seed. But if it dies, it produces many seeds. Anyone who loves their life will lose it, while anyone who hates their life in this world will keep it for eternal life" (John 12:24–25, NIV). These words of Jesus are very hard to follow, but I believe it is particularly difficult in the West, being as we are enamored from this world with all his comforts, pomp and glory, particularly those of us who are placed in positions of power. Romero advocated for the essential. As a true prophet his harshest words were reserved for the rich, but it was a compassionate call for conversion.

In the words of iconic musician Bob Marley, "How long shall they kill our prophets, while we stand aside and look? Some say it's just a part of it. We've got to fulfill di book." Romero stands in the tradition of Martin Luther King Jr., Mahatma Gandhi, Dietrich Bonhoeffer, Thomas Becker, and all the prophets of Israel, and just as it happened with his predecessors, his longings remain unfulfilled. Romero, however, is the closest to us and the more relevant. Born in a modest family, he grew up more apolitical than conservative; a faithful son of the church, but he foresaw the chaos that would be caused by unbridled neoliberalism and the primacy of money, most painfully felt in the regions used as pawns, in the geopolitical conflict between the superpowers.

We live in a time of crisis, now exacerbated by a viral plague, but the worst plague is a perennial crisis of inequality, hedonism, and aggression against the most vulnerable members of society, often manifested sexually, as the #MeToo movement has painfully demonstrated. Romero's traumas and psychological impairments did not prevent him from taking *the big step,* of giving himself up to God's will even at the cost of his life. In the middle of it all he was a man of prayer and developed a deep spirituality, which allowed him to cross the threshold. The last words he pronounced when offering the eucharistic elements were: "May this body immolated and this blood sacrificed for humans nourish us also, so that we may give our body and our blood . . . not for self but to impart notions of justice and peace to our people."[9] Seconds later a shot was heard, and Romero crossed into a different dimension.

A PRAYER/ORACION

Dios Padre de todos los hombres
Que nos diste en tu siervo Oscar Romero
A un pastor fiel y celoso
Fervoroso amante de tu iglesia
Y en ella de los pobres y los mas necesitados
Concedenos como el vivir conforme al Evangelio de
   tu hijo Jesus
Y otorgame por su intercesion el favor que te pido.
   Amen.

God and Father of all
You gave us in your servant Oscar Romero
A zealous and faithful pastor
Intensely loving of your church
And in it of the poorest and the most needy
Grants us, like him, to live according to the Gospel of
   your son, Jesus
And bestow on me through his intercession the favor
   I ask. Amen.

Published by the Archdiocese of El Salvador (translation mine).

NOTES

Introduction

1. Transference is here understood as attributing certain qualities to an individual simply by the fact that they possess a title or position that suggests such qualities; counter-transference refers to the analyst's (in this case the writer's) emotional or ideological response to the individual under study.
2. Robert Jay Lifton, in *Whose Freud? The Place of Psychoanalysis in Contemporary Culture*, ed. Peter Brooks and Alex Woloch (New Haven, CT: Yale University Press, 2000), 222, 223.
3. Ibid., 223
4. Later in this work I will refer to Jean-Paul Sartre's definition of this concept. It is worth noting that Sartre was not a believer and his concept was purely philosophical.
5. Freud did not elaborate much on the concept of countertransference but was aware of the phenomenon. He saw it as the patient's influence on the unconscious of the analyst. That is why he emphasized the need for the analyst himself to be thoroughly analyzed in order to recognize his own biases and emotional tendencies and be able to use his unconscious toward the patient, as a receptive instrument, thus being able to discern what the patient's unconscious is communicating.

Chapter 1: Ways of Seeing Romero

1. The term *aggiornamento* refers to the effort of the Roman Catholic Church to come to terms with the modern world.

2. Historical materialism is the premise of Marxism that desig-
nates material reality as the basis of everything, including
consciousness.

3. πρᾶξῖς • (prâxis)

4. Jürgen Moltmann, "European Political Theology," in *The
Cambridge Companion to Christian Political Theology*, ed. Craig
Hovey and Elizabeth Phillips, Cambridge Companions to
Religion (Cambridge: Cambridge University Press, 2015), 3–22.

5. See Paulo Freire, *Pedagogy of the Oppressed*, 30th anniversary ed.
(New York: Bloomsbury, 2000).

6. The scorched-earth policy had been previously used in Vietnam.
It consisted in killing an entire village—men, women and
children—suspected of collaborating with the guerrillas. My-Lai
was the most notorious example in Vietnam; El Mozote, in El
Salvador. The soldiers also killed the villagers' livestock and
destroyed their crops and other means of subsistence. American
advisers were often detected at the scene.

7. The Brazilian educator Paulo Freire is among the most influential educational thinkers of the late twentieth century. Born
in Recife, Brazil, on September 19, 1921, Freire died of heart
failure in Sao Paulo, Brazil on May 2, 1997. Following the military coup d'etat of 1964, he was jailed by the new government
and eventually forced into a political exile that lasted fifteen
years. In 1969 he was a visiting scholar at Harvard University
and then moved to Geneva, Switzerland, where he assumed
the role of special educational adviser to the World Congress
of Churches. He returned to Brazil in 1979. Freire's most well
known work is *Pedagogy of the Oppressed* (1970). Throughout
this and subsequent books he argues for a system of education
that emphasizes learning as an act of culture and freedom. He
is most well known for concepts such as "banking" education,
in which passive learners have preselected knowledge depos-
ited in their minds; "conscientization," a process by which the

learner advances towards critical consciousness; and the "culture of silence," in which dominated individuals lose the means by which to critically respond to the culture that is forced on them by a dominant culture.

8. Gustavo Gutiérrez, *A Theology of Liberation* (New York: Orbis, 1988). (Originally published in Lima in 1971.)

9. Jon Sobrino, *Christology at the Crossroads: A Latin American Approach* (London: SCM Press Ltd., 1978).

10. Ignacio Ellacuria, *Freedom Made Flesh: The Mission of Christ and His Church* (New York: Orbis, 1976).

11. J. L. Segundo, *The Liberation of Theology* (New York: Orbis, 1976).

12. Fidel Castro and Frei Betto, *Fidel y La Religion [Fidel Castro and Religion]* (Habana: Consejo de Estado, 1985).

13. Leonardo and Clodovis Boff, "A Concise History of Liberation Theology," *Introducing Liberation Theology* (New York: Orbis, 1987). http://www.landreform.org/boff2.htm

14. Pedro Trigo, *Creation and History* (New York: Orbis, 1991).

15. Otto Maduro, *Marxismo y Religión* (Caracas, Venezuela: Monte Avila Editores, 1978).

16. *The Challenge of Basic Christian Communities*, ed. Sergio Torres and John Eagleson, trans. John Drury (New York: Orbis, 1982).

17. *The Idols of Death & the God of Life: A Theology*, Pablo Richard et al. (New York: Orbis, 1983).

18. J. Miguez Bonino, *Doing Theology in a Revolutionary Situation* (Philadelphia: Fortress Press, 1985).

19. Enrique Dussel, *A History of the Church in Latin America Colonialism to Liberation (1492–1979)*, trans. Alan Neely (Grand Rapids: Wm. B. Eerdmans, 1981).

20. The term "base communities" refers to the small groups of workers, peasants, and unemployed people who gathered together to pray, study the Bible, and apply their conclusions to their living conditions.

21. Gustavo Gutiérrez, *We Drink From Our Own Wells: The Spiritual Journey of a People* (Maryknoll, NY: Orbis, 1984), 15.

22. Gutiérrez, *A Theology of Liberation*, 284, note 51.

23. *Expanding the View: Gustavo Gutiérrez and the Future of Liberation Theology,* ed. Marc Ellis and Otto Maduro (New York: Orbis, 1990).

24. Vatican II, also called the Second Vatican Council, was a gathering of cardinals, bishops, and the pope that took place in Rome from 1962 to 1965 and was heavily influenced by liberal theologians.

25. James R. Brockman, *Romero: A Life* (New York: Orbis, 1989).

26. Jesús Delgado, *Oscar A. Romero Biografía* (Madrid: Ediciones Paulinas, 1986).

27. There is a great deal of debate among Romero's biographers as to whether his transformation from a conservative priest to a radical bishop can be called a conversion in the traditional sense of the word. The conventional meaning of conversion is that of moving from a state of sin into one of righteousness. But conversion can also be seen as a change in identity, such as the case of Saul, a persecutor of the church, becoming Paul, the apostle. This kind of transformation could also apply to Romero as it included all major aspects of his life and action and suggests the pattern of what has traditionally been described as conversion.

28. Jon Sobrino, *Monseñor Romero* (San Salvador: UCA Editores, 1997).

29. The book has been translated as Maria Lopez Vigil, *Oscar Romero: Memories in a Mosaic* (Washington, DC: Epica 2000). I read the book both in Spanish and English. I have used the authorized translation for the purposes of this review.

30. Placido Erdozain, *Archbishop Romero: Martyr of El Salvador* (New York: Orbis, 1984).

Notes

31. Salvador Oña Carranza, *Romero—Rutilio: Vidas Encontradas* (*Romero—Rutilio: Convergent Lives*), not translated (San Salvador: UCA, 1992).
32. Zacarias Diez and Juan Macho, *En Santiago de Maria Me Tope con La Miseria: Dos Años en la Vida de Monseñor Romero (1975–1976) Años del Cambio?* [*In Santiago de Maria I Stumbled into Misery: Two Years in the Life of Monseñor Romero (1975–1976) Years of the Change?*], not translated. Publisher unknown.

Chapter 2: Childhood and Youth

1. Liisa North, *Bitter Grounds: Roots of Revolt in El Salvador* (Toronto: Between the Lines, 1981), 20
2. Any of a number of philosophies maintaining that a knowledge of God may be achieved through spiritual ecstasy, direct intuition, or special individual relations, especially the movement founded in 1875 as the Theosophical Society by Helena Blavatsky and Henry Steel Olcott (1832–1907). From *Oxford Dictionary of Phrase and Fable* (New York: Oxford University Press).
3. It is commonly acknowledged, as a joke, that the conquest of Mexico was done by the Tlaxcaltecs who joined forces with Hernan Cortes to defeat their enemy tribe, that is, the imperialistic Aztecs.
4. *History of El Salvador, Volume II.* Ministry of Education, El Salvador (San Jose: UCA, 1982).
5. Thomas P. Anderson, *Matanza: El Salvador's Communist Revolt of 1932* (Lincoln: Univ. of Nebraska Press, 1971), 1.
6. As told to Maria Lopez Vigil, *Memories in a Mosaic,* 16.
7. Ibid.
8. A possessor of the evil eye.

9. Bishop Martin Barahona, personal testimony.
10. Delirium tremens (also called DTs) is the most dangerous form of alcohol withdrawal. It occurs in about one out of every twenty people who have withdrawal symptoms. In delirium tremens, the brain is not able to smoothly readjust its chemistry after alcohol is stopped. This creates a state of temporary confusion and leads to dangerous changes in the way your brain regulates your circulation and breathing. The body's vital signs such as your heart rate or blood pressure can change dramatically or unpredictably, creating a risk of heart attack, stroke, or death (Harvard Medical Schools Consumer Health Information).
11. Gaspar Romero, personal communication.
12. Janet Geringer Woititz, *Adult Children of Alcoholics* (Pompano Beach, FL: Health Communications, 1983).
13. Scrupulosity, or religious OCD (obsessive compulsive disorder), is a condition that has been observed as far back as the 1600s. Individuals suffering from this form of OCD become excessively fixated on certain aspects of moral or religious doctrine, to the detriment of their overall well-being.
14. When I was a Roman Catholic seminarian in San Salvador in the early sixties some spiritual counselors still recommended the *cilicio* as a sure way of keeping sexual desire in check. At the time, the reforms of the Second Vatican Council were just beginning to be implemented and the teaching at seminary was clearly Neoplatonic, emphasizing the irreconcilable struggle between flesh and spirit. In psychoanalytic terms the *cilicio* could be construed as a symbolic castration device as applied to an arm or a leg. The wearing of it was at any rate a drastic measure to subdue the competing desires of the flesh. In psychoanalytic terms we would say that it was a way to keep aggression and libido in check or, in fact, to turn it against oneself, with sado-masochistic implications.

15. Responding to an offense, real or imagined, by doing the contrary; that is, expressing allegiance instead of anger to offending parties.
16. A psychological mechanism geared to transform energies attached to negative feelings into positive ones, such as service to God and neighbor.

Chapter 3: Ministry and Martyrdom

1. Octavio Paz, *The Labyrinth of Solitude: The Other Mexico* (Mexico: Philanthrophic, 1985).
2. Jesús Delgado, *Oscar A. Romero Biografía*, 28 (translation mine).
3. Maria Lopez Vigil, *Memories in a Mosaic*, 21, 22.
4. Ibid., 29.
5. Ibid., 23.
6. Ibid., 30.
7. Ibid., 31.
8. Ibid., 31.
9. The Opus has been greatly maligned particularly since the publication of *The Da Vinci Code*, wherein a "monk" of the Opus Dei is portrayed as a sinister conspirator. The Opus, however, does not have monks. It is composed of priests and laypersons who sometimes take religious vows but they are all encouraged to live in the world and influence political, educational, and religious institutions.
10. Kristin Rosekrans, personal communication.
11. Delgado, *Oscar A. Romero Biografía*, 41
12. The corresponding psychiatric diagnosis is obsessive compulsive disorder (OCD).
13. Brockman, *Romero: A Life*, 50.
14. Ibid., 40.
15. Ibid., 41, 42.

16. Maria Lopez Vigil, *Memories of a Mosaic*, 31–32 (translation mine).
17. Delgado, op. cit., 32.
18. Fr. Mario Benitez, private conversation.
19. Quoted in Zacarias Diez and Juan Macho, *En Santiago de Maria Me Tope con La Miseria*, 43 (emphasis in the original; translation mine).
20. Maria Lopez Vigil, *Memories in a Mosaic*, 37–38, 40.
21. Martin Barahona, personal communication.
22. Sigmund Freud, *The Future of an Illusion*, vol. XXI, *Standard Edition of the Complete Psychological Works* (London: Hogarth, 1953).
23. James R. Brockman,"The Spiritual Journey of Oscar Romero," *Spirituality Today*, vol. 42, no. 4 (winter 1990): 303–322.
24. See introduction.
25. Maria Lopez Vigil, *Memories in a Mosaic*, 52.
26. Quoted by Brockman, *Romero: A Life* , 55.
27. Ibid., 55.
28. Fr. Juan Macho in Maria Lopez Vigil, *Memories in a Mosaic*, 71.
29. Diez and Macho, *En Santiago de Maria Me Tope con La Miseria*.
30. Juan Macho in Maria Lopez Vigil, *Memories in a Mosaic,* 76.
31. Martin Barahona, personal communication.
32. Ernestina Rivera in Maria Lopez Vigil, *Memories in a Mosaic*, 103.
33. Salvador Carranza in Maria Lopez Vigil, *Memories in a Mosaic*, 99.
34. Antonio Fernandez Ibanez in Maria Lopez Vigil, *Memories in a Mosaic*, 112–113.
35. Inocencio Alas in Maria Lopez Vigil, *Memories in a Mosaic*, 116.
36. Inocencio Alas in Maria Lopez Vigil, *Memories in a Mosaic*, 117–118.
37. In El Salvador the blanket lay terminology for many emotional ailments like compulsivenes and anxiety is "nerves."

38. Anonymous, *Rutilio Grande* 1st. ed. (UCA: San Salvador, 1978), 25 (translation mine).

39. Mother Luz Cuevas, personal communication.

40. *Monseñor Romero: A Mystery of God* (San Salvador, 2004), videotape.

41. Rogelio Pedraz in Maria Lopez Vigil, *Memories in a Mosaic*, 132.

42. Oscar Romero, homily, April 30, 1978 (translation mine).

43. Oscar Romero, homily, May 7, 1978 (translation mine).

44. Ruben Zamora in Maria Lopez Vigil, p.194.

45. Carlos Cabarrus in Maria Lopez Vigil, p. 212

46. Brockman, *Romero: A Life*, 109–115.

47. Ibid., 110.

48. Oscar Romero, private diary, 1993, 23–24.

49. Brockman op. cit., ibid.

50. Brockman, *Romero: A Life*, 113, 114, 115.

51. Jean-Paul Sartre, *Dirty Hands* from *Three Plays by Jean-Paul Sartre (Dirty Hands, The Respectful Prostitute, and The Victors)*, trans. Lionel Abel (New York: Alfred A. Knopf, 1948).

52. Matthew 16:24

53. Oscar Romero, private diary, March 19, 1978, 47.

54. Oscar Romero, homily, January 13, 1980 (translation mine).

55. Oscar Romero, homily, March 16, 1980 (translation mine).

56. Margarita Herrera in Maria Lopez Vigil, *Memories in a Mosaic.*, 308.

57. Rafael Urrutia in Maria Lopez Vigil, *Memories in a Mosaic*, 322.

58. Maria Lopez Vigil, *Memories in a Mosaic*, 147.

59. Ibid., 148–49 (translation mine).

60. A deep sense of guilt, combined often with feelings of numbness and loss of interest in life, felt by those who have survived some catastrophe. It was first noticed among survivors of the Holocaust. Survivors often feel that they did not do enough to save those who died or that they are unworthy relative to the perished. *The New Dictionary of Cultural Literacy*, 3rd ed., 2002.

61. Oscar Romero, homily, March 23, 1980 (translation mine; caps in the original).
62. Vatican Council "The Church in the Modern World," 39.
63. Oscar Romero, homily, March 24, 1980 (translation mine).

Chapter 4: A Life's Conclusion

1. Anna Peterson, *Martyrdom and the Politics of Religion: Progressive Catholicism in El Salvador's Civil War* (Albany: SUNY Press, 1996), 98.
2. Latin saying: "The voice of the people is the voice of God."
3. Mamerto Romero, personal communication.
4. The superego is the psychological component that stores the rules and commandments instilled by society and the family.
5. See Richard Isay, *Being Homosexual: Gay Men and Their Development* (New York: Vintage Books, 2009).
6. See Maria Lopez Vigil, *Memories in a Mosaic*, 31.
7. Brockman, *Romero: A Life*, 50.
8. Dr. Johan Noordsij, personal communication.
9. Mother Luz Cuevas, personal communication.
10. We do not understand masochism completely, but we know it does not necessarily involve sexual pleasure; in this case masochism may be seen as the undertaking of suffering to expiate, or triumph over, adverse circumstances by means of self-immolation.
11. Mary Jones, *Epiphany: The Psychology of Joyce's "The Dead."* An essay hosted by Literature Classics.com, https://www.classics-network.com/essays/epiphany-the-psychology-of-joyces-the/332
12. Jean-Paul Sartre, *Critique de la Raison Dialectique* (Paris: Gallimard, 1960).
13. Peterson, *Martyrdom*.
14. Oscar A. Romero, *The Violence of Love,* trans. James R. Brockman (Maryknoll, NY: Orbis, 2004).

15. Matthew 11:12 KJV.
16. Peterson, op. cit., 112.
17. "For you died to this life and your real life is hidden with Christ in God" (Colossians 3:3 NLT).

Chapter 5: Finding Resonance

1. As referenced in chapter 1, transference is here understood as attributing certain qualities to an individual simply by the fact that they possess a title or position that suggests such qualities; countertransference refers to the analyst's (in this case the reader's) emotional or ideological response to the individual under study.
2. Salvador Barraza, personal communication.
3. Report from the Conferencia Episcopal Latino Americana (Latin American Bishops Conference), Medellin, Colombia, 1968.
4. A Roman Catholic Synod recommended ordaining married men in remote places of Amazonia but Pope Francis finally vetoed the measure. In his recent book, Pope Emeritus Benedict XVI argues for celibacy as a gift to the church. See: Benedict XVI and Robert Cardinal Sarah, *From the Depths of Our Hearts: Priesthood, Celibacy and the Crisis of the Catholic Church* (San Francisco: Ignatius Press, 2020).
5. With the release of *The Da Vinci Code* this device has become peculiarly popular to the point that the New York headquarters of the Opus has been flooded with numerous calls by people who want to join the order and subject themselves to their disciplines. The sadomasochistic overtones are hard to ignore.
6. Martin Barahona, personal communication.

Postscript

1. Colossians 3:5.
2. Meaning "Indians." In reality, only 1 percent of pure indigenous descent are left while the majority are mixed, but many have Asian features and are regarded disdainfully by the Caucasian elite.
3. Carlos Dada,"How We Killed Archbishop Romero," *El Faro*, March 25, 2010, https://elfaro.net/es/201003/noticias/1416/ How-we-killed-Archbishop-Romero.htm.
4. Ibid.
5. McCarthyism, named for Senator Joseph McCarthy, is the term describing a period of intense anticommunist suspicion in the United States that lasted from roughly the late 1940s to the mid-to late 1950s. McCarthyism is also referred to as the Second Red Scare.
6. Former US Ambassador Robert White admitted he is not sure of the first name of the Muyshondt revealed by the source which strikes one as an egregious, perhaps intentional, mistake.
7. Matthew 19:24. The Jewish Talmud also uses that expression; it seems to refer literally to a very narrow entry into Jerusalem where camels could barely fit.
8. See 1 Corinthians 1:23.
9. Romero's Final Homily, March 24, 1980.

BIBLIOGRAPHY

Documentation on Archbishop Romero

Brockman, James R. *La Palabra Queda: Vida de Mons. Oscar A. Romero.* San Salvador: UCA, 1985.

Delgado, Jesus. *Monseñor Romero.* San Salvador: UCA, 1998.

Díez, Zacarías. *En Santiago de María me Topé Con la Miseria: Dos años de la vida de Mons. Romero; 1975–1976, años de cambio?* 1994.

Romero, Oscar A. *Monseñor Romero: Sus cartas personales, pensamientos, y consejos; En el XV aniversario de la muerte de Monseñor Oscar Arnulfo Romero.* 1917–80.

———. *Voice of the Voiceless: The Four Pastoral Letters and Other Statements.* 1985. New York: Orbis, 2020.

———. *The Violence of Love: The Pastoral Wisdom of Archbishop Oscar Romero.* New York: Harper & Row, 1988.

———. *Archbishop Oscar Romero: A Shepherd's Diary.* Cincinnati, OH: Saint Anthony Messenger Press, 1993.

Methodology

Freud, Sigmund. "Recommendations to Physicians Practicing Psycho-Analysis." *The Standard Edition of the Complete Psychological Works of Sigmund Freud.* London: Hogarth, 1953–1974.

Bibliography

Gay, Peter. *The Freud Reader.* New York: W.W. Norton, 1989.

Luhrmann, T.M. *Of Two Minds: The Growing Disorder of American Psychiatry.* New York: Knopf, 2000.

Suleiman, Susan R. "Introduction: Varieties of Audience-Oriented Criticism." *The Reader in the Text: Essays on Audience and Interpretation,* eds. Susan R. Suleiman and Inge Crosman. Princeton: Princeton Univ. Press, 1980.

Tompkins, Jane P. *Reader-Response Criticism: From Formalism to Post-Structuralism.* Baltimore: Johns Hopkins, 1980.

Runyan, William M. *Life Histories and Psychobiography: Explorations in Theory and Method.* New York: Oxford Univ. Press, 1984.

Socioeconomic and Historical Analysis

Anderson, Thomas. *El Salvador 1932. Los Sucesos Politicos* (El Salvador 1932. The Political Events). San José: EDUCA, 1976.

Castro, Rodolfo Baron. *La Población de El Salvador* (The Population of El Salvador). San Salvador: UCA, 1978.

CEPAL. *El Salvador: Notas Para el Estudio Económico de América Latina* (El Salvador: Notes for the Economic Study of Latin America). México, D.F. 1977.

Carpio, Salvador. *Secuestro y Capucha* (Torture and Kidnapping). San José; EDUCA, 1979.

Dalton, Roque. *El Salvador.* La Habana: Enciclopedia Popular, Monografia, 1965.

Dunn, John. *Modern Revolutions. An Introduction to the Analysis of a Political Phenomenon.* Cambridge: Cambridge Univ. Press, n.d.

Gilly Adolfo. *Guerra y Política en El Salvador* (War and Politics in El Salvador). México: Nueva Imagen, 1981.

Gonzalez, Ignacio. *La Batalla de El Salvador* (The Battle of El Salvador). Ediciones Prolibro, México: Nueva Imagen, 1981.

Bibliography

Report of the Latin America Bureau. *Violence and Fraud in El Salvador.* London, 1977.

Report of the Latin America Bureau. *El Salvador Bajo el General Romero: Un Análisis de los Primeros Nueve Meses del Régimen del Presidente Romero* (El Salvador Under General Romero: An Analysis of the First Nine Months of the Regime of President Romero), London, 1978.

Religion and Society

Boff, Leonardo. *Cry of the Earth, Cry of the Poor.* Maryknoll, NY: Orbis, 1997.

Garcia, Ismael. *Justice in Latin American Theology of Liberation.* Atlanta: John Knox, 1987.

Dussel, Enrique D. *History and the Theology of Liberation: a Latin American Perspective.* Maryknoll, N.Y: Orbis Books, 1976.

Gutiérrez, Gustavo. *A Theology of Liberation: History, Politics, and Salvation.* Maryknoll, N.Y.: Orbis, 1988.

Gutiérrez, Gustavo, Ellis, Marc H., Maduro, Otto. *The Future of Liberation Theology: Essays in Honor of Gustavo Gutiérrez.* Maryknoll, NY: Orbis, 1989.

Ruether, Rosemary Radford. *Liberation Theology: Human Hope Confronts Christian History and American Power.* New York: Paulist, 1972.

Psychohistory

Coles, Robert. *The Mind's Fate: A Psychiatrist Looks at His Profession: Thirty Years of Writings.* Boston: Little, Brown and Company, 1995.

Derrida, Jacques. "The Purveyor of Truth." *Yale French Studies*, 52. New Haven: Yale, 1975.

Bibliography

Fisher, David James. *Cultural Theory and Psychoanalytic Tradition.* New Brunswick, NJ: Transaction Publishers, 1991.

Holland, Jay N. *The Dynamics of Literary Response.* New York: Oxford Univ. Press, 1968.

Lacan, Jacques. *Ecrits: A Selection.* London: Tavistock Publications, 1980.

Lesser, Simon O. *Fiction and the Unconscious.* Chicago: Chicago University, 1957.

Loewenberg, Peter. *Fantasy and Reality in History.* New York: Oxford Univ. Press, 1995.

Roazen, Paul. *Erik H. Erikson: The Power and Limits of A Vision.* Northvale, NJ: Jason Aronson, 1997.

Loewenberg, Peter. *Decoding the Past: The Psychohistorical Approach.* New Brunswick, NJ: Transaction Publishers, 1996.

Mazlish, Bruce. *The Leader, the Led, and the Psyche: Essays in Psychohistory.* Hanover, NH: University Press of New England, 1990.

Meissner, W. W. *Ignatius of Loyola: The Psychology of A Saint.* New Haven: Yale Univ. Press, 1992.

Wright, Elizabeth. "Modern Psychoanalytic Criticism." In *Modern Literary Theory*, eds. Ann Jefferson and David Robey. London: Batsford, 1982.

Vernant, Jean Pierre. *Passe et Present: Contributions a Une Psychologie Historique. Storia e Letteratura.* (Edizioni di Storia e Letteratura) 88–189. Roma: Edizioni di Storia e Letteratura, 1995.